T. LYTTON

DRINK IN ME

The True Timmy

By

Timothy D. Lytton

1

DRINK IN ME

T. LYTTON

Table of Contents

FORWARD . . . . **P 5**

GLASS #1 . . . . **P 11**

GLASS #2 . . . . **P 19**

GLASS #3 . . . . **P 29**

GLASS #4 . . . . **P 37**

GLASS #5 . . . . **P 51**

GLASS #6 . . . . **P 65**

GLASS #7 . . . . **P 87**

GLASS #8 . . . . **P 103**

GLASS #9 . . . . **P 115**

GLASS #10 . . . . **P 127**

GLASS #11 . . . . **P 145**

GLASS #12 . . . . **P 161**

GLASS #13 . . . . **P 175**

GLASS #14 . . . . **P 187**

GLASS #15 . . . . **P 197**

LAST CALL . . . . **P 205**

3

DRINK IN ME

T. LYTTON

FORWARD SMELL & TASTE

"There is no greater agony than bearing an untold story inside you." - Maya Angelou

Somehow, this book ended up in your hands. I am sure you either stumbled upon it by accident, heard about it, and felt a bit of morbid curiosity, or you are in prison, and the only two options on the book cart were either this or "Free on the Inside!" Whatever the case may be, you're in luck because I have quite an unbelievable story to tell you, one I'm confident will capture your intrigue, and at the very least, you will find it entertaining. It is an intimate narrative about my life story and how I've become the person I am today.

Who am I, you ask? No one special, no one famous. I haven't invented a billion-dollar company, gone from rags to riches, broken any world records, or have an earth-shattering secret that can change your life. I am just one of billions of people in the world who each have their own stories to pour out and let everyone else drink in, and this is just one of them.

We all have an interesting story to share, and we all carry our own cross to drag and bear.

Everyone's process is the same: you're born, you live some years, and then you die. While the born and die parts of life are universal for every human, there is only one birth and one death, but it is the living of life that separates each person and creates a snowflake life that is unique to no one else.

DRINK IN ME

Like every snowflake that falls from the sky, our lives and experiences are all very different, and our snowflakes are shaped by a combination of what we actively choose to do for ourselves and reacting to what other people do to us. However, as you will soon discover, my snowflake has been strewn and shaped by some harsh, extraordinary, and incredible things along the way.

My story is a unique one; it's a heartbreaking and messed up one that may, at times, seem too far-fetched and unbelievable to be real. It has a little bit of everything that makes a train-wreck hard to turn away from, and you might think it's a Hollywood script or some B-rated movie.

Occasionally, I find myself wishing it were merely a made-up movie. But, sadly, sometimes life can be more intense and depressing than any fictional story or lousy movie. Just as the adage goes, truth can indeed be stranger than fiction.

For this reason, do not worry about offending me by questioning what I am writing because, if I had not lived it, I would find it dubious at best. It is all true, though, and one of the best things about the truth is it never changes.

We all know that there are always two sides to every story, and unfortunately, people only know the wrong side of mine. And that's not right, or fair. So, this book is my attempt to set the record straight and offer my side of events, and let the reader decide.

But before we take this little stroll down my memory lane and before I get intimate and share my very personal thoughts, feelings, and secrets with you, we need to set the foundation and expectations for our new relationship as a writer and reader. Do you see how I carefully said, "writer and reader" instead of "author and reader"? Let us be upfront and clear with each other from the start; I am no author.

T. LYTTON

I am not even a writer, but I must define this book in some way. I did not graduate from college with a degree in literature or writing, and I have never written anything more than high school essays and letters to friends and family. Therefore, if you are hoping for a sophisticated book and a masterpiece of fine literature, I am very sorry to disappoint you. This book is probably closer to *The Jerry Springer Show* than *Shakespeare.*

So, instead of expecting to read your typical book, imagine us kicking back and having a casual chat and a friendly conversation and drinks over a few glasses of beer, tea, wine, coffee, weed, or whatever is your thing. If you can read my story in this way, we will get through this as smoothly as possible.

Here soon, you will understand why I did not get the opportunity to go to college, and who knows, I may have missed out on becoming a great author.

Basically, if you lower your expectations for me now, you might not be disappointed and possibly let down later.

I apologize in advance. This is my flaw and what I lack to bring to our new relationship, along with money and good looks. But, if my lack of writing skills and broke ass is not a deal-breaker and you are still intrigued enough to continue for now, let me assure you I do have some positive attributes I can offer in our relationship. I have a job, my own car, and I'm loyal. Plus, I will be open and honest with you. This part of my life will be like a literal open book to you.

I kind of have no choice. No matter how embarrassing, shameful, or crazy parts there are to this story, I will be honest. I have nothing to hide, so let's go ahead and rip this Band-Aid off now. For the last 25 years, I have had to live my life marked as a sex offender and have been unfairly judged as one of the worst kinds of human beings.

DRINK IN ME

The truth has not been known, and I have had to bear the consequences of my silence. Not because of shame or guilt but silence due to fear. I have personally experienced the destructive impact people in positions of power and authority can have, and if you have ever been abused or violated by authorities, you know how paralyzing and helpless it is. However, I know who I am and what I am not.

I will be the first to admit I am only human and have made mistakes, and I am not even close to being perfect. And I can own up to and take responsibility for the actual and real mistakes I have made in my life.

Likewise, I will not hold back the responsibility for those who have committed criminal acts and misdeeds against me. It is one thing when a regular person commits a crime, but when someone in a trusted authority does it, it magnifies it exponentially.

The people whom this book is about have incomprehensibly wrecked my life, damaging my reputation by unjustly labeling me as a sex offender since I was 18 years old.

At that age, I was seriously outmatched, like stepping into the boxing ring with a 20-year-old Mike Tyson. My life got messed up as badly as my face would get messed up by Tyson.

But if I had to box Mike, I would at least try and throw a punch or two before he knocked me out. This book is my attempt to throw a punch back. I want to fight as best as I can with everything I've got. So why now, you might ask?

The answer is that I have reached a point in my life where I do not have much left to lose.

Nearly everything worth living for has been taken away, and I am left with one option or choice. To write this book, clear my name, and tell my side of this tragedy. If I don't, everyone will only know the lies and believe I'm some sex offender and villain.

The reality is I am just an ordinary guy, no different from any other respectable and decent man.

And the best way I can show the world the truth is to expose myself in the right way, share some of my most personal, intimate memories, and let everyone drink in a few glasses full of Timmy Life and hope they can stomach it. So, here's to revealing the truth and to my brother Ricky, Cheers.

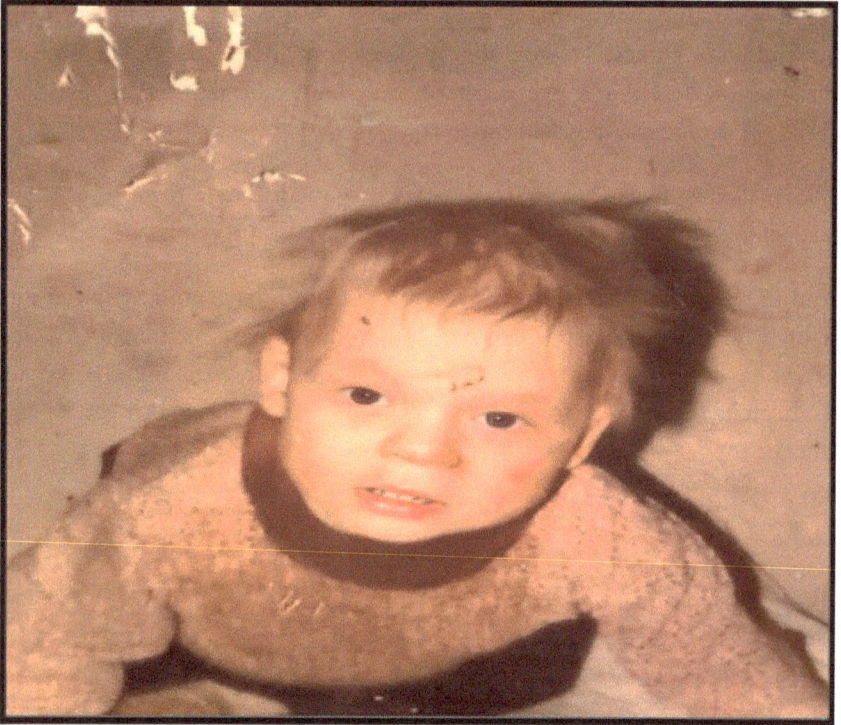

This is not a child you can sponsor.

This is the only baby picture I have, and a great way to get you prepared for what you are about to read. Enjoy...

GLASS #1:

"Family is not an important thing. It's everything." – M. J. Fox

On Sunday, March 16, 1980, in the small town of Statesville, North Carolina, I, Timothy Daniel Lytton, was born, weighing 12 lbs.

This caused me to get stuck coming out of my mother's vagina, which, after having five kids already, should have been well-attuned to handling my big ass. She said the doctor had to cut her from pink to stink to get my broad shoulders out. This, in turn, made my mother bleed so much that she said she almost bled to death, and I nearly drowned in her blood.

I guess you can say from literally my first moments in life that I've had to "Rock it out" and struggle to do things the hard way. I was the sixth of seven kids to pop out of my mother, Diane. She was not your typical Pisces, speaking without a filter or shame, and she seemed to enjoy being the center of attention.

She took pleasure in trying to shock people with her words and observing their reactions to her peculiar behavior. I believe she derived a different kind of satisfaction from intentionally embarrassing others. In total, she had five daughters and two sons. Growing up, I was surrounded by women, including my two grandmothers, one aunt, and two nieces.

All my sisters had different personalities, and they were all beautiful women. My oldest sister, Wendy, was 13 years older than me and was a Scorpio with dark hair.

DRINK IN ME

When I was six years old, I was the ring bearer at her wedding. She married a guy named Bobby, and soon after, they had two girls, Kim and Tiff, making me an uncle before I turned 10. Wendy had a bold character and was not afraid to speak her mind. She loved the attention and was the type of person who would openly point out a giant pimple on someone's forehead for everyone to hear as if they were unaware of it. After Wendy was born, Diane met Wayne Lytton, a Scorpio and the man of her dreams.

They quickly became pregnant. It's clear they both liked to bump the dumplings, judging by the number of children they had. The story goes when Diane discovered she was pregnant for the first time with Wayne's child, she went to him and said, "I'm pregnant, and you're the father, so now you have to marry me." It was an unconventional way to get engaged, but it suited them well. Following that, Diane and Wayne hurriedly arranged their wedding before anyone noticed Diane's pregnancy.

They managed to get married just in time, and shortly after the wedding, Christie, the first member of Wayne and Diane's team, was born. Christie was nine years older than me and had always been a wonderful older sister. She was a Sagittarius with a quiet yet sweet and timid nature. Christie was incredibly generous and had a caring and gentle attitude, particularly toward animals. However, she could also be quite emotional and sensitive. A little over a year later, my sister Mary-Jane, with her tanned skin, black hair, and the gift of gab, was born.

Whenever anyone wanted to know the truth, they could always turn to Mary. She was a Cancer sign, and her roller-coaster of emotions could make her shift from calm to storm in the blink of an eye. Mary-Jane loved to talk and flirt with her charm. She also had a compassionate nature and a big heart, and she was always protective of her family. About another year and a half later, Joann, our other sister, followed.

Jo, as we all called her, was a Leo sign, and like a lion, her loyalty was fierce. She was born with a severe case of cerebral palsy and had to undergo six major back surgeries by the age of 18. She was one of the strongest people I knew. She was there to help me whenever I needed it. Like all the other girls, Jo was blessed with beauty. She had dark hair and a soft, smooth complexion.

It seemed like every guy who met her would fall in love and try to date her. Three years later came my brother Ricky, who was a Cancer like Mary-Jane, and like most Cancers, he had quick mood swings.

Being only three years older than me, he was the primary male figure in my life, filling the role a father was supposed to. Rick was very intelligent, and growing up, he was athletically gifted. He often teased me but also had a great sense of humor. Instigating drama and stirring things up out of boredom were some of his character traits. Three years after Rick was born, I was born. I was the only kid Wayne wasn't there for during the birth, and I guess this might be why he couldn't stand me.

At the age of 1, he gave me the only broken bone in my life. He threw me against the wall and broke my nose. Of course, I don't remember it, but Diane and Mary told me I wouldn't stop crying, and as everyone knows, the best way to get a baby to stop crying is to knock them out. Right? Sounds logical.

I am a full Pisces, Sun, and moon, with Taurus rising. Whether you believe in astrology or not, you cannot help but see the uncanny accuracy in how it describes someone's personality traits. I am, in fact, a logical and practical person and would be the first to question the veracity of Sunday's paper horoscope. But I have also wondered why so many different people share the same personality traits and how they seem to fit perfectly with their astrological signs.

DRINK IN ME

I figured there must be some truth or something that has allowed humans to keep using and studying it for thousands of years. Nikola Tesla and Manly P. Hall, two of history's intellectual giants, both had a connection to astrology.

Tesla used astrology as inspiration in his innovative work, while Manly P. Hall, an esoteric scholar, believed in astrology, seeing it as a tool for understanding the human psyche.

I cannot deny the accuracy with which they describe a Pisces personality, and it is precisely how I am as a person. I'm a calm, laid-back, easy-going guy, and I have so much empathy and compassion for human beings and animals.

I treat everyone the way I want to be treated. The golden rule should be the easiest to follow. I do not bother anyone, and I keep to my own business. I value my privacy like a fish values water. I believe in fairness, equality, and the precept of live and let live. I got to be the baby for a while because Jennifer, my youngest sister, came when I was three.

She was also a Pisces, and as we grew up together, I spent a lot of time with her. Her nickname was Bull, and she used to play football with me and my male friends in the yard until she hit puberty. Like all my sisters, Jennifer was sweet, kind, and beautiful, always there for me whenever I needed them.

After my sister Jennifer was born, I fell into this no man's land. I wasn't the oldest, I wasn't the first-born son, and I was no longer the baby. I was just number six. Navigating family dynamics and growing up in a less-than-ideal environment set the stage for some of the more complex and challenging experiences of my childhood. Like when I was four years old.

At the time, we lived in a small apartment that had been divided from a large house into two separate units. Next to our apartment was another one, where an elderly woman named Kiddy lived with her two adult delinquent sons and a daughter.

Tommy, Kiddy's son, was an overweight and drunken bully. He was as unintelligent as he was mean-spirited. Diane, being the ever-so-caring mother that she was, not only allowed Tommy to bully and push us around but also let us roam the apartments unsupervised. Kiddy, on the other hand, was a complete dumbass.

She used to keep a little .38 revolver lying on the back of her couch's headrest. One day, tired of being picked on by Ricky, I walked next door and sat on the couch. Kiddy was in another room, and no one else was around, so I reached my arm up, feeling around until my hand found the gun. I hopped off the couch, gun in hand, and headed straight for Ricky. When I saw him, I pointed the gun at him and said, "Bang-bang." I can't remember if I pulled the trigger or not, but the gun was loaded. So, luckily, I didn't actually shoot my brother.

Of course, I was only four years old. I wasn't trying to hurt him—I just wanted him to finally be scared enough to stop picking on me. I mean, seriously, who the hell leaves a loaded handgun on the back of their couch, knowing there are kids running around? I can't imagine living that down if something terrible had happened.

As crazy as that sounds, it was just another day in my young life. My childhood was a roller-coaster of WTF moments, and one particularly vivid memory stands out in the chaos that was my everyday life.

DRINK IN ME

As a kid, I was a little unconventional. I used to run around outside naked in the winter and wear thick coats in the summer. I have no idea why, but somehow, that weird little quirk helped protect me from serious injuries.

When I was five years old, my brother and I were playing outside on a summer day. I had my head down, busy moving rocks with a toy dump truck, when a car backed out of our driveway and ran over me—trapping my foot underneath. The woman driving wasn't paying attention and kept backing up, completely unaware that she had just run over a little kid.

I can't remember if I screamed, but even if I did, she didn't hear me. Luckily, my brother saw what happened. He rushed toward the car, leaped onto the hood, and started pounding on it, shouting, "You ran over my brother!" That finally got her attention. After dragging me for what felt like forever, she finally stopped. They had to lift the car to free me. Then, before the ambulance even arrived, the woman just drove away.

Thankfully, despite having scratches on my face and a nasty road rash on my hands, my injuries weren't severe—because I was wearing a thick winter jacket. If my brother hadn't noticed what was happening, I don't know if I'd even be alive right now. These two experiences—almost shooting my brother and almost getting run over to death—are some of my earliest and most memorable moments.

And they set the stage for a life that would continue to be anything but ordinary. Little did I know, these incidents were just the beginning of a journey that would challenge me in ways I never could have imagined.

Joann 10, Mary-Jane 11, Timmy 4, Ricky 7, 1984.

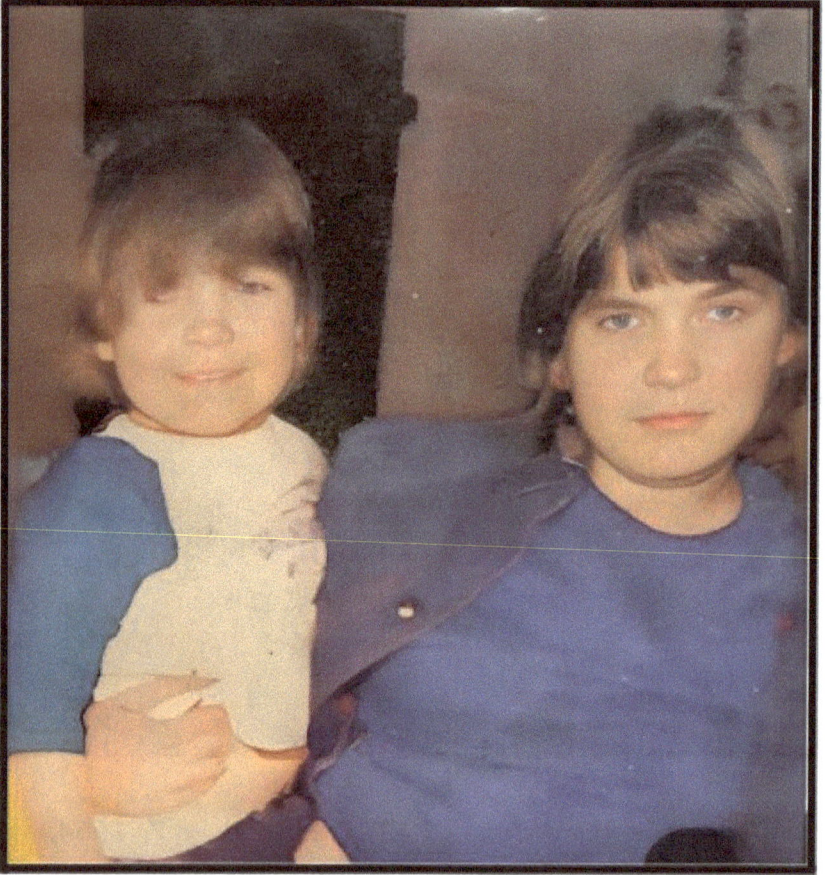

Jennifer 3, Christie 15, 1986

GLASS #2:

"The beautiful thing about learning is that no one can take it away from you." - B.B. King

My mother had to almost drag me into school on my first day of kindergarten because I was so bashful and nervous. Even at the early age of five, I had anxiety and felt physically awkward. I told her I did not want to go because I was extremely shy and would hide behind her whenever I met someone for the first time. My mother tried to reassure me by telling me there would be a bunch of toys and other kids to play with, and I would have fun and make lots of friends. But the thought of all those strangers in an unfamiliar place terrified me even more.

The one good thing my mom was halfway right about was I met my best friend, Mikey, who is still my best friend to this very day. My mom and I walked into Mulberry Street Elementary School and Ms. Chambers' kindergarten classroom. With wide eyes, I clung onto my mom's shirt, looking around at all the children, laughing, playing, yelling, running, and hearing how loud it was.

Taking in the chaos, I turned to my mother and said, "Nope," and I told her I was ready to go back home. She sat at one of the small round tables and said, "Let's just give it a minute." She pointed to the toy section of the classroom and said, "Oh, look at all the toys." As we were poor, I didn't have a lot of toys at home, so even though I tried my best, I couldn't resist.

She told me to find a toy to play with and assured me she would be right there the whole time. Slowly, I made my way to the toys, constantly looking back to make sure she was still there.

At some point, I got lost in my own little world, intensely examining the toys, until the teacher instructed all the kids to sit on the floor in front of her chair. I thought to myself, "Not today." I turned to the table where my mother had been sitting—only to find she was gone. It took me a few more seconds to comprehend what had happened. I had been tricked. I was alone in a room full of strangers.

I immediately had a full-blown panic attack and bolted for the door. I ran out into the huge four-way hallway, crying and desperately looking around for my mom. I wanted to run, but I had no idea where to go, so I just stood there in the middle of the hall—lost and sobbing.

Ms. Chambers came up behind me, trying to soothe me, but when she put her hands on my shoulders, it only made me freak out even more. I do not like people I don't know touching me—especially when I'm upset.

I don't know why my brain works the way it does, but I've never been a toucher, and when I'm distressed, the last thing I want is for someone to put their hands on me. Anyway, I started freaking out so badly that the teacher had to go get my sister, Joann, from another classroom.

She was in one of the higher grades, and they brought her in to calm me down. When I went back to the classroom, I still refused to sit with the other kids, and I sat on the floor in the back corner by myself. It had nothing to do with the other kids; I just felt so betrayed. I remember sitting in the corner feeling better with my back against the wall, and my arms crossed almost all day.

It wasn't until later that afternoon that I finally emerged from my self-imposed exile and started playing with the toys. That's when I met Mikey. We started playing with little Hot Wheels cars and decided to build a ramp to launch them into the air and make them crash into each other.

Our plan worked a little too well—one of the cars flew across the room and crashed into the teacher's leg. When she asked who did it, neither of us said a word. So, naturally, we both got punished and were sent to the corner.

Which was fine with me. I just went back to the same corner I had been in all day. Since that day, Mikey has been the best friend a guy could ask for. He is always loyal and there when I need him. Mikey is a Scorpio, and it turned out we had a lot in common. Like me, he came from a big, dysfunctional family—his parents had nine kids (seven boys, two girls), and his dad was an abusive alcoholic, just like mine.

The only difference was that Mikey's dad was a lot smaller. We were always there for each other when one of us was mistreated, forming a strong friendship based on support and understanding. Growing up, everyone at school called us brothers. Eventually, Mikey and I got so tired of explaining that we weren't actually related that we just started telling people we were cousins.

It was way easier than having to explain our friendship over and over again. In the years that followed, we became inseparable. We did everything together—riding bikes, roaming the neighborhood, and, of course, causing trouble. Most of it was harmless. Some of it? Not so much.

When we couldn't find something to do, we would create our own games, like "Roof ball," or build clubhouses in the woods, filling our imaginations with excitement. Throughout our childhood, Mikey was the one person who truly understood me, and I knew he would always be by my side. However, behind the facade of this close friendship was the harsh reality of my family life.

My family was poor and were welfare recipients all my life. Sometimes, Jo and I would sit on the porch and wait for the mailman on the 1st of the month to deliver the packet of food stamps.

DRINK IN ME

Food stamps used to come in an envelope and looked like Monopoly money. I hated using paper food stamps in stores, as it would make me stand out and embarrass me.

It was rough growing up poor as shit, having to wear baggy hand-me-downs that were already used before Ricky got them. Which meant it was more like hand-me-down downs. On top of Wayne's abuse and the lack of encouragement and motivation at home, compounded with being the poor kid at school, it seemed like there was no hope.

Overall, we had a dysfunctional family, and I could tell you so many disturbing stories about my childhood it would make you cringe and want to cry.

I don't think my parents, Diane and Wayne, ever really wanted kids, let alone wanted to take on the responsibility of raising so many. Neither of them had any ambition to work good jobs. Diane was too lazy to work and instead preferred to use a woman's unique power to hustle men out of their money.

She had a talent for lying—she was a pro at conning all types of guys, either over the phone or through handwritten letters. While Wayne was at work, she spent her days running her little scams, playing men like a fiddle. Wayne, on the other hand, worked off and on at different wood mills and lumber yards.

But he wanted to keep his money for himself or blow it all on alcohol, drugs, and hookers. He was a big guy—physically strong from all the hard labor jobs he did. Ricky used to say a good bit of Wayne's strength came from something called Dumb-Dumb strength. He was 6'3" and 345 lbs. of pure dumb-dumb strength. His deep, growling voice was booming loud and intimidating as hell. Wayne's abusive, alcoholic, control-freak behavior caused me and my siblings to suffer a lot of abuse.

It didn't help that Diane couldn't keep from running around with any and every man. When Wayne caught her being unfaithful, he used it as an excuse to get drunk and beat the shit out of his kids—especially me and Ricky. Whenever he beat Ricky, Ricky wouldn't cry—which only made Wayne angrier, so he beat him even more. Whenever he beat me, I would cry—so he beat me more for crying. It was a no-win situation with him.

Me and Ricky would sit up at night and talk about how, when we got bigger; we would beat his ass. He was always quick to anger and would dictate everything we did, including what games we could play and who we could play with. He even gave each of us nicknames and refused to call us by our real names.

Wayne would love to get drunk and give everyone a hard time. His idea of a Friday night movie snack wasn't popcorn or chips, instead, it was raw cabbage, sardines, and buttermilk that would make you gag. Whenever he pretended to be a parent, it was just to control or harass us, and it seemed more like entertainment for him.

I recall one day when I was 7 years old, Ricky and I were outside, and Ricky was trying to teach me how to ride a bike. Wayne was, as usual, drinking and decided to teach me how to ride by pushing me toward some metal trash cans down a hill. Of course, he would get angry if you didn't figure it out on the 3rd try and would slap you across the head or push you even harder and faster the next time.

Wayne would get angry if you could not learn anything within a short amount of time. He would live with us from time to time, constantly popping in and out of our lives, and when he was in, he would do more abuse and control than parenting. Diane was around and would sometimes get beaten, too, but a lot of the time, she wanted us to stay out of her way and leave her alone.

DRINK IN ME

Wayne's abuse took many forms—each one seemingly designed to chip away at our sense of safety and self-worth. Here is a glimpse into what Wayne thought was parenting. Sometimes, when Wayne was drunk and wanted to terrorize someone, he would make me get a book and read it to him.

I was only seven or eight years old and still learning to read. I hated reading to him because he was so intimidating and would already make me nervous. With Wayne, you could not stutter or stumble on your words, or it would piss him off, and he would smack the back of your head. Not lightly, either. I would always try to grab a book I already knew, or that was easy to read. This one day, though, I think Wayne had it in for me or was extra drunk because he made me get a hard book from my grandmother's bookshelf.

I started reading, and somewhere along the way, I started stuttering and stumbling at some of the big words. I came to a word I could not read and was stuck. Wayne got pissed and barked the word at me while he slapped the back of my head hard. I tried to keep reading as tears started to build up in my eyes, and it was hard to see the words.

I was fighting back the tears, trying to keep reading, and Wayne was getting annoyed because, for whatever reason, I was not allowed to cry, ever. With my eyes full of tears and now my nose starting to run, when some tears or snot fell on the book, it sent Wayne over the edge.

He snatched the book from my lap, held it in front of my face, and yelled, "Look at this nasty shit!" and smashed the open book in my face with his other hand behind my head like you see when someone smashes a pie in someone else's face. He slung the book on the floor and slapped the back and side of my head again. This time, it was so hard that I flew forward and landed headfirst on the floor. Luckily, my forehead caught my fall.

I do not know whether he knocked me out for a second or hitting the floor headfirst made me dizzy, but I was slow to sit up, and all I could see were black and white dots. Wayne was yelling at me to "Grab the goddamn book and get up." I could barely see because of the tears and black dots, so I just started feeling around on the floor for the book.

I am reaching around, trying to hurry and find that damn book because when Wayne tells you to do something, you have to jump to it right then. Wayne gets up and slaps the back of my head again, hard enough to see even more dots, and grabs my shirt at the collar. He slides me like a fuckin' bowling ball across the floor and right into the wall. My back hit the wall, and I was still dazed, my vision was still a little blurry, but I saw the book right beside me.

He told me to "Get up and take the goddamn book to my room." I guess I wasn't getting up fast enough because he came over to me, grabbed my shirt again at the collar, jerked me up, walked me to the living room door, and shoved me hard out into the hallway right into the hallway wall, causing me to fall back down on my ass.

I think my falling aggravated him because he huffed, "Goddamn it," and came up to me and gave me one more extra hard slap to the side of the head and jerked me up with two hands by my shirt and pants, and carried me over to the bedroom door, throwing me like a fuckin' bale of hay across the entire room and onto the bed while I'm still clutching the book in my arms.

This is just one of many similar stories from my childhood. By now, you can probably get a good idea of what life was like for my siblings and me during those years. I remember the cops were never any help. They would show up, make Wayne leave, and that was it. He'd be gone for an hour or two, only to return and pick up right where he left off.

DRINK IN ME

Eventually, we stopped calling the law and started calling my Grandma Headrick—Diane's mother. My grandma, Ethel Headrick, was an Aries, 4'10" tall, and maybe 100 lbs. soaking wet. She may have been a small package, but so is TNT—and she was just as explosive. True to her zodiac sign, she was a little firecracker. She was also the only person who put real fear into Wayne. And every time, she scared him off.

How could a small, older lady like Ethel run off a 6'3", 345 lb. man? Simple. She always came armed with two small .22 caliber revolvers. Wayne knew Grandma wasn't afraid to shoot him—either on purpose or by accident. You see, Grandma's hands would shake when she pointed the guns, so it wouldn't take much for her to accidentally pull the trigger.

Whenever Wayne went on one of his drunken rampages, we would lock him outside and call Grandma. She would pull up in her car, step out with her pants yanked up to her bosom, and those two revolvers stuffed in her waistband.

Wayne would try to run his mouth—but in the end, he always went to his car and left. I would stand at the window, watching. I loved seeing someone finally put fear into him for a change. Grandma would stand there, hands on both guns, as if daring Wayne to give her a reason to finally pull the trigger.

One time, I even heard her tell him, "No jury would ever find me guilty for putting a bullet in your head." CPS was called a few times because of the abuse, but nothing was ever done. I remember Diane cussing out one of the CPS workers, pushing him down the porch steps, and yelling at him until he got in his car and drove away—never to return. It was like CPS didn't want to do anything. They always made sure to point out that if they took us away, my siblings and I would be separated and placed in different homes. But my siblings were the only good and positive thing in my life.

Yet, even amid such wishful fantasies, one particular real day stands out, bringing me back to the harshness of my life. When I was about nine years old, I played outside with Ricky and Mary-Jane. We wanted to build something for our Grandma Lytton in the yard, and we found a pile of what we thought was scrap wood, bricks, and wire next to an old wooden shed behind our house on Hill Street. Mary had a bunch of plastic flowers and suggested we build a cross, so we started working on it.

I grabbed a board from the pile and tried to stick it in the ground, but it was not deep enough. I saw a cement block in the pile and decided to use it to drive the board into the ground. However, after a few hits, the cement block broke and split in two. Suddenly, Wayne's loud and commanding voice interrupted us from somewhere in the distance behind me. Wayne was in the house, sitting on the couch with the back door open. He asked who had broken his block and demanded that the culprit come forward.

My whole body froze in fear, and I started shaking as I wished I could turn back time. Ricky quietly wondered how the hell Wayne could hear us. Mary and I looked up at the house's back door, but no one was standing there. Wayne's voice got louder and angrier, and my panic intensified. I thought about running away but knew it would only worsen things. I looked at Mary and Ricky, but no one said a word. I slowly let the two halves of the broken block fall to the ground, and, with trembling legs, I turned to face my fate. That's when Ricky spoke up and took the blame for breaking the block. He walked past me, went up the back steps, and into the house.

Mary and I stood there, tears streaming down our faces while listening to the sounds of Ricky being beaten by Wayne. I felt incredibly guilty for letting Ricky take the blame for my mistake, and I sat under a nearby tree for the rest of the day, feeling like a coward and a terrible person. Ricky never came back outside that day, and the memory of that moment haunted me for years to come.

TIM 12, RICKY 15, 1992

GLASS #3:

"What lies behind us and what lies before us are tiny matters compared to what lies within us." – Ralph Waldo Emerson.

As a kid growing up in our unique family dynamic often left me retreating into my own thoughts. Whenever Wayne was living with us he did not allow my brother, sisters, and me to have friends. Because of this, we had to play with each other or find something to do on our own. So I spent a lot of time in my own head. Especially whenever I was beaten, I would check out from what was happening and think about anything I could to escape reality.

One of my favorite things to imagine was floating in outer space, weightless and alone in the vast emptiness. I would fantasize about flying around and visiting each planet from afar, like a satellite passing by and admiring its calm and colorful beauty. In space, everything is quiet and peaceful. I would close my eyes and try to imagine what it would feel like to be weightless, both physically and emotionally. Sometimes, a heart can feel as heavy as the entire body.

I had to find a way to be content and happy inside my head and mind. I floated alone, quite calm and peaceful, without loud yelling and with no one around to hit me. This proved to be a good and useful quality as I grew up. Even today, when I find myself in a situation with nothing but my thoughts to keep me company, I can sit and contemplate the nature of the universe, attempting to formulate a unified theory that reconciles quantum mechanics and general relativity.

DRINK IN ME

I do not consider myself smart or intelligent, and I know the chances of me solving the problem are about one in the total number of stars in the sky, essentially impossible. Nevertheless, this does not stop me from getting lost in thought about it.

I can allow myself to ponder other difficult questions life must ask, such as where humans come from, whether ghosts and aliens are real, and why women are so difficult to understand. I may never find the answers to these questions, but they help to occupy my mind when needed. My tendency to withdraw mentally extended beyond home and into my school life.

I had a habit of daydreaming a lot in school and gazing out the window during class, hardly ever speaking. It was difficult to focus on math, science, or any other subject when you had to think about going home and getting beaten for any and no reason. This used to confuse my teachers.

When I was about eight years old, in third grade, they suggested placing me in Special Ed, thinking I had learning issues, even though my grades were perfectly fine. They even questioned whether I might be cheating or guessing my way through exams all because I preferred not speaking and daydreaming instead of actively participating. I spent the latter part of that year in Special Learning.

The following year, when I was in fourth grade, my new teacher had a different opinion. She believed I belonged in the Advanced Learning program with exceptionally bright kids. It was a sudden shift, and I found myself among the "gifted" students.

But this didn't last long. The additional workload, attention, and after-school commitments associated with the program proved too much for either of my parents to manage. Consequently, I was pulled out and placed back into the regular class.

The whole experience was a bit taxing and left me confused for a while. I always tried my best not to attract attention and to be as invisible as possible. Strangely enough, being quiet, keeping to myself, and daydreaming seemed to draw the attention I strive to avoid.

Personally, I have always been on the shy side. Being the center of attention or having all eyes on me was never something I wished for. I would never dare to raise my hand in class, even if I knew the answer to a question.

Whenever it was my turn to read aloud or perform a task that required everyone's focus on me, I would find a way to bypass it or do it as quickly as possible to divert the attention elsewhere. I was always the quiet kid who said little and remained alone. I prefer to sit and watch people and their behavior. I am not referring to the creepy type of staring but the curious observation of people-watching.

Often, I would lose myself in my thoughts, which sometimes made me appear distant or aloof. This tendency to observe rather than participate sometimes led to unexpected situations. In 5th grade, my preference for people-watching landed me in hot water with a girl named Jessica.

Our class was taking the end-of-year test, and the teacher had all the desks turned in different directions so no one could cheat, and my desk ended up right in front of Jessica. As I took the test, I found myself stuck on a question, so I started to stare off into space to think about it. Jessica was wearing bright, neon pink knee-high stockings and a white skirt.

She was rocking each leg back and forth, and the movement caught my eye. When I looked over at her, she stopped moving with her legs wide open. I was trying to make out what I was seeing. She was wearing white panties, and I would have immediately looked away, but what caught my eye and made me do a double-take was the red spots on them.

DRINK IN ME

Having five sisters, I learned early in life that when the moon is right, girls bleed down there for a few days a month. At first, I thought maybe she was bleeding. I couldn't make out what it was until she slowly opened her legs even more. That is when I noticed they were hearts. She was wearing white panties with red hearts. When I realized she was not bleeding, I looked up, and our eyes met. She looked at me with narrow eyes but an eerie, calm expression. She stared at me while she twirled her hair with two fingers.

I think she had been looking at me the whole time because she raised her hand and made this insidious smirk with her lips until the teacher came up to her. I saw her whisper something to the teacher, and the teacher looked right at me in shock.

She came right over to me and grabbed me by my ear, jerked me up, spun my desk around to the corner, and sat me back down. She whispered to me I should be ashamed of myself. That was the first time I was left with the horrible feeling of being blamed for something not right. I was like 10 years old.

I did not look at girls that way at that age. The teacher embarrassed me in front of the entire class and tried to punish me by shaming me. Besides, I didn't even like Jessica.

I only had one crush throughout all my years in school. Her name was Carolyn, and she was part of the 'rich kid's crew' but was not stuck up like the rest of them. She was always so nice and friendly. She and I were in the same classroom up until high school. I would sometimes get stuck looking at her in class. Not the stalker stare, but the mesmerizing, admiring gaze people have when they see a beautiful painting in a museum. I couldn't help it; she was so nice to look at I didn't realize I was even looking. One year, she had gotten braces on her teeth, and when she talked, she would get these little bubbles in the corners of her mouth, which I thought were cute.

.

I remember the first time she spoke to me. It was in kindergarten, and one day, as I was playing by myself, she walked over, handed me a Ken doll, and said,

"Here, you can be my husband; she has a husband, and I don't have one. I need you to go to work every day like he does." I guess she was playing house, and she pointed in the direction of some other little boy and girl. I sat there for a moment, holding the Ken doll, looking at her, unsure of what to do. She didn't wait for me to decide, though. She directly and demandingly told me to "Come on," and marched away.

I got up without saying a word, followed her to where she and the other kids were playing. I remember standing there, not knowing what to do. She was so clean and neat; her hair was always combed and styled perfectly, and her personality was strong and confident.

At that age, I was like every other little boy, and I did not like girls or want to play with them. I thought they were the enemy and gross, Yet Carolyn's presence stirred something in me, a feeling I couldn't quite comprehend. She was the first girl to make my heart race, the first to give my belly that weird feeling.

I thought she was so disgustingly beautiful. The second time Carolyn spoke to me was in 3rd grade when we were about 8 years old. Our class had to performed a play, and after the play while the adults were chatting and people were leaving, Mikey and I decided to embark on a little adventure.

We started climbing the upside-down L-shaped basketball goal, feeling invincible. I had made it to the part that holds the backboard and rim, feeling pretty proud of myself, when I heard a small voice from behind and below me say, "Tim, is that you?" I looked down and saw Carolyn standing there, her eyes wide with concern. Suddenly, my hands felt sweaty, and my feet seemed to forget how to grip the metal pole.

DRINK IN ME

She warned me, *"Be careful, you're going to fall!"* I thought to myself, 'Yup, now I am.'

It wasn't just the physical danger of falling that worried me; it was the mortifying thought of looking clumsy in front of Carolyn. At that moment, I was acutely aware of how high up I was, how ridiculous I must look, and how much I wanted to impress this girl who rarely noticed me.

The other time she spoke to me was when I was in the 5th grade, and Mikey was having "one of those difficult days," like we all have, for whatever reason. He had climbed on top of the school roof at lunchtime, and he was cursing the gym teacher and tossing things off the roof. All the kids were at the cafeteria window, looking out and laughing. When I went to the window and found out what was going on and that it was Mikey up on the roof, I told the teachers to let me go outside and talk to him.

They said it was too dangerous because he was throwing projectiles off the roof. So I had to sit at the lunch table by myself, where me and Mikey would usually sit and watch as all the other kids were laughing and talking shit. I guess Carolyn saw me sitting alone, so she came over and gave me a pear. I'm not sure why it was a pear, but I thought it was nice of her.

She asked me what was wrong with Mikey. All I could say was, "I don't know?" I didn't know what was going on. I ended up keeping that pear until it finally rotted away. Whenever they got Mikey to come down off the roof, he had to go to a hospital for about two months, and it left me lost and alone every day.

Some kids sent Mikey a get-well-soon card, and Carolyn was one of them. She was a nice person, and that is why I liked her. Of all the girls in school, Carolyn was the only one who made me nervous and self-conscious. Mikey has a younger brother named Terry, who is a year younger than us.

T. LYTTON

All of us went to the same school, and every school year, Mikey, Ricky, Terry, and I would debate who the prettiest girl in school was. They would name a different girl every year, while I would choose Carolyn each year. I got teased, and they would give me hell about it, but in my defense, she seemed to get more beautiful with each passing year.

In high school, I finally worked up the nerve to write Carolyn a letter expressing how I felt and ask if she would go on a date with me. I was so nervous; I had spent a whole week rewriting the letter over and over until I was satisfied. What I was left with was a 4-page long confession letter that held all my shy desires, every wishful longing, and my entire heart and the only way I knew how to explain or tell her how I felt.

I knew trying to speak to her verbally would have been a disaster. On that day, I still had to keep wrestling with myself to work up the courage to give it to her. I even went by the horticulture class garden, and I stole one of their prettiest flowers and almost got caught. When it was time for lunch, I threw the letter away, only to make myself go back and get it out of the trash before the end of lunch. The only time I saw her each day was right after my lunch.

It's when I knew I could catch her leaving gym class as I was supposed to be heading into the gym. After lunch, I stood outside the gym with my letter and stolen flower, my heart pounding, my hands sweaty, my knees shaking, trying to keep from passing out.

Unfortunately, for some reason, Carolyn came out of gym class crying and walking with two of her girlfriends. Of course, it would have been a bad time to try and hand her my heart, so I ended up throwing the letter away and never got the chance to tell her how I felt or never knowing what her answer would be. Soon after, she moved away, and I never saw her again.

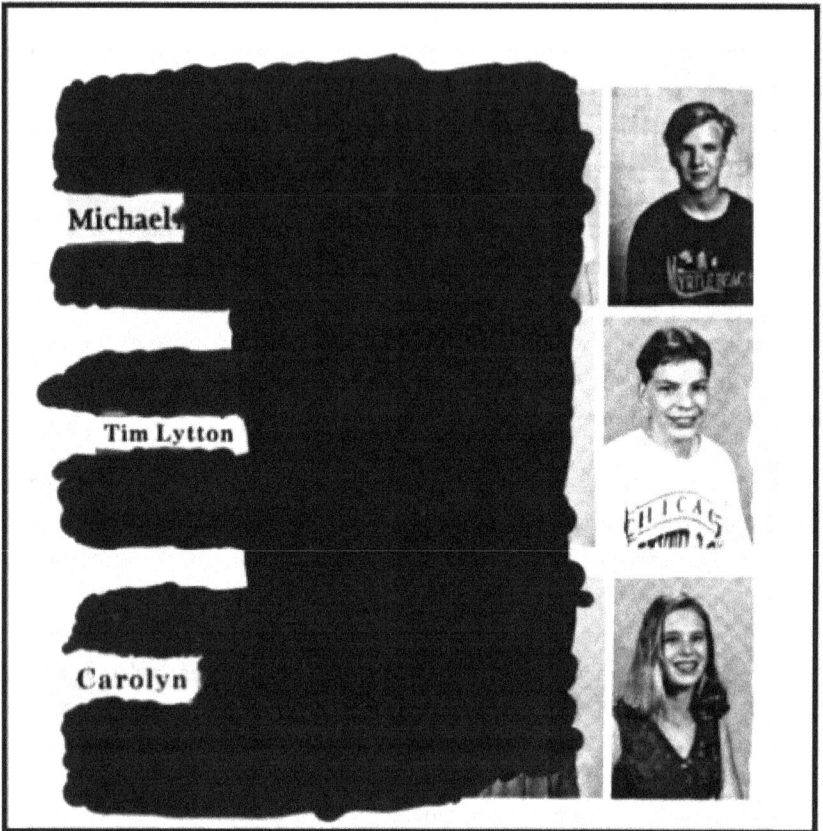

Michael

Tim Lytton

Carolyn

Timmy 15, Mikey 15, Carolyn, High School Yearbook.

GLASS #4:

"Adolescence is a border between childhood and adulthood. Like all borders, it's teeming with energy and fraught with danger." - Mary Pipher

When I was about 12 years old, Wayne put his hands on me for the last time and moved out of the home for good. He would still stop by the house occasionally to try to control things. After Wayne's departure, Diane raised us alone with little care for what we did.

We could go anywhere and do anything if we did not bother her or cost her any money. We lived in an old white house on Hill Street, a place that was barely holding itself together.

The porch sagged in places, and the paint had long since chipped away, leaving faded patches of gray underneath. Inside, the floors creaked with every step, and the windows let in drafts so strong we often joked it was colder inside during the winter than it was out.

The house had been under renovation by the landlord for as long as we could remember, but progress was slow and inconsistent. That's probably why we got to stay there at such a cheap rent.

The landlord had promised to fix things up, but aside from the occasional patch of fresh plaster on the walls or new tiles in the bathroom, it still felt like the place was crumbling around us. There was a half-finished look to everything: doors that didn't quite shut right, and walls that were partially stripped for repainting but left untouched for months.

DRINK IN ME

Despite the state of disrepair, the house had one thing going for it—a huge yard and a patch of woods out back, which became our playground. I was able to have friends visit so Mikey, Terry, Ricky, and I hung out every day, much to the annoyance of my sisters. During the summer, it was as if they practically lived at my house. We would play Nintendo or football in the yard.

It turned out that Mikey only lived a block away so it was easy to walk from my house to his. Halfway between my house and Mikey's was a charming girl named Angie, the same age as us. With her pale skin and long brown hair, she was one of the prettier girls in the neighborhood, and she knew it. Angie was a little queen in her world, and her personality was loud and cocky. During the warm spring and summer days, Angie would often sit on her porch, listening and singing along to her radio, and would usually stop me and Mikey whenever we walked by. At first, Angie was just a friend to us, someone we enjoyed looking at and talking to while we strolled down the street.

But one day, as I was on my way to Mikey's house, she stopped me on her porch, and we talked for what seemed like hours. When it was time for me to leave, Angie revealed something that caught me off guard.

"I really like you more than just a friend," she confessed softly, her eyes sincere. *"I know Mikey has a crush on me, but I don't feel the same way about him. And I don't want to hurt his feelings. So, can we just keep this between us? Please?"*

I may have been young and inexperienced, and my naivety made me an easy target for her words, but I was not immune to flattery or the sense of pride from getting attention from the opposite sex. Angie was the first girl to say she liked me in any way or expressed any interest in me, and her words worked like a charm. I didn't want to hurt my best friend, and I didn't want to jeopardize my newfound connection with her.

So, I played along with what she told me for a whole week or two. But one day, as I walked to Mikey's house, I saw him sitting on the porch swing with Angie, and they were a little too close to each other, laughing and talking. I walked up to the porch, and Angie started acting weird and insisting that she had to go inside her house. Confused and hurt, I asked Mikey what was going on.

"Angie and I like each other, more than just friends," he admitted. *"We didn't want to hurt your feelings, Tim."*

I couldn't believe it; it was the same bullshit Angie had told me. Mikey and I started arguing, which led to pushing, which led to us fighting in the middle of Angie's front yard.

Well, it was more like a frustrating, angry submission wrestling match because neither of us wanted to hurt the other. We fought on the ground until we were both tired and gave up. Covered in dirt and grass and breathing hard, we went to Angie's bedroom window together and told her she must pick.

Angie's bedroom window was right by the front porch and yard, and she had stood there the whole time, watching us, and maybe even liked it. We told her she had to pick, and with some serious "Girl-attude", she rolled her eyes, smacked her lips, crossed her arms, lean-dropped to one hip, stood in her window, and said,

"I can't pick." She said, *"Timmy, you're so cute and sweet, and you think I'm pretty, and Mikey, you're fun and exciting, and I can talk to you. I like you both, and if y'all were smashed together into one person, y'all would make the perfect guy."*

I said, *"Whatever, I'm going home,"* I started walking back to my house.

DRINK IN ME

A few minutes later, Mikey ran behind me to catch up, and we talked. We realized she had been lying to both of us with the same story. She is the only girl Mikey and I ever fought over. We made a pact and a promise never to fight over any girl ever again, and to this day, we never did.

Angie, however, was so angry at both of us that she went around calling us names and talking shit about us to the other kids we all knew. That was my introduction to girls, and as frustrating as the situation with Angie had been, it didn't leave any lasting scars on me or my friendship with Mikey. We quickly moved on to new adventures—most notably, our regular Saturday night trips to the skating rink.

It was a treasure trove of pretty girls, and I would watch in amazement as Ricky, Terry, and even Mikey, who was almost as shy as I was, effortlessly approached them, making it all look so easy. Fueled by determination, I eventually mustered the courage to try it, thinking to myself, "Why not? I can do this." Every time, I would take a deep breath, swallow my shy, and walk up to a girl I liked, attempting to strike up a conversation.

Regrettably, things never went as smoothly for me as they did for the others. Somehow, I always managed to turn the interaction into a cringe-worthy, awkward affair, not just for me but for the poor girl as well. I could make the girls smile and giggle, just as Ricky advised, but the laughter didn't seem to be shared "with me"; more often than not, it felt aimed "at me."

Even worse, I'd sometimes be met with those bewildered "WTF" expressions laced with a hint of pity from the girls. I convinced one girl to join me for a couple's skating, which unfortunately ended with me stumbling and taking her down with me, leaving her with a gashed elbow. There was the time I accidentally spilled a rainbow snow cone on a girl with her white shirt and shocked her with the ice.

It seemed the more I tried, the more excruciatingly awkward the encounters became. Eventually, I abandoned the cold approach and began exploring alternative methods, like writing notes.

Despite my mishaps at the skating rink, I remained hopeful. My adventures in the world of dating were about to take an intriguing turn with my very first "official" girlfriend and heartbreak when I was 12 years old. Her name was Heather, and she lived next door to Ricky's girlfriend, Laura, and her sister, Katie.

When Ricky first started dating Laura, he introduced me to Katie. Since they were sisters and we were brothers, it would have been cool, but Katie and I did not click. Katie was 14 and pretty, with blond hair, and had developed breasts at her age.

She and I talked for a few weeks, but there was something off about her I could not figure out. Something that did not feel stable or relaxing. She wasn't mentally slow or mean to me; she was nothing like that; she was just intense and a little unpredictable. She would do some off-the-wall shit for no reason and without warning.

One time she was pissed, and she started banging her forehead on a brick wall so hard you could hear the thuds and could feel the concrete floor vibrate. Therefore, her personality and my personality did not go well together.

Even at that age, I was as laid back and easygoing as I am today, and I like smooth and calm women. Plus, Katie was bigger than I was physically and might have been able to whoop my ass at the time, so I told her nicely that she was a cool girl, but we were too different. But I told her I had the perfect guy for her, someone who was a great person and could match her crazy energy.

DRINK IN ME

She and Mikey hit it off great and became a couple, no problem. Laura and Katie had a friend named Heather who lived right next door. She was fourteen, about to turn 15, and one day, while Ricky, Mikey, and I were hanging out at Katie and Laura's house, I was introduced to Heather.

She was fair-skinned, had long light brown hair, and she, too, had well-developed breasts. I felt like a runt. I hadn't even started my growth spurt yet. Everyone around me was bigger, taller, and weighed more than me. Even the girls and Heather were no exception.

Heather and I started talking, and when she told me her age, she also mentioned that she could not date anyone younger than her. Or they could only be a year younger but had to at least be a teenager. When she asked how old I was, I naturally said 13.

So, I told a little lie, but get how ridiculous and silly this shit was. Mikey is only four months older than me. His birthday is in November, and mine is in March. When I met Heather, it happened to be early November, and Mikey had just turned 13.

Technically, everyone around me was a teenager except me. I was four months behind. I figured in four months, what the hell, I'll be 13, no big deal. I told everyone, Rick, Mikey, Laura, and Katie, what I had told Heather and asked them to go along with me.

And everyone did for a while. All of us would go to the movies together or meet at the park to hang out or hang out at Laura and Katie's house.

Everything was good for about a month. Heather and I would kiss at the movies but only pop kisses and not a lot because I used to have to stand on my tiptoes to kiss her.

Whenever she and I would be standing around, like in front of the movie theater, I would always try to stand on the curb and have her stand in the parking lot so she and I would be about the same height. I think the height difference may have made her feel weird, too.

But for some reason, she would rock it out with my short, undersized self. She was from a wealthy family, and I thought I was the man until one fine day, she called me on the phone and said,

"You are only 12 years old. You lied to me, and I am dumping you. Your brother told me the truth."

I felt the weight of the world crashing down on me. The pain was overwhelming, and for the first time, I understood what a broken heart truly felt like. This was in January, so I was only two months from turning thirteen.

Looking back, it seems dumb, but the hurt was real. Ricky's excuse for ratting me out was that it was for my own good, and it was only a matter of time before she broke my heart anyway. Ricky said,

"She's a rich girl, and you're a poor boy, and that never works, so stop fuckin' crying, and never cry over any bitch ever. Never give your heart to a bitch, and always be able and ready to drop a bitch for a new one at any time."

I knew that was terrible advice back then, and besides, I do not have the heart to use someone like toilet paper and treat anyone like shit for no reason. I knew he was just angry that she broke my heart.

Although I knew Ricky's harsh perspective on relationships wasn't his true feelings, my experiences continued to shape a trial-and-error path for me, one that was about to become even more personal and formative.

DRINK IN ME

Another one of life's lessons learned unexpectedly and in Timmy style was when I was thirteen and I learned how to kiss. Mikey's older sister, Bernadette, was the girl who taught me how to French kiss.

We would all hang out sometimes: Mikey, Terry (their older sister), Bernadette, Ricky, Mary, and Jo. We would sit around, listen to the radio, talk, and play games. One day, we somehow got to playing either truth or dare or a game that somehow led to me having to kiss Bernadette.

Of course, I said I did not know how to kiss with an open mouth or a French kiss. I guess she felt brave enough to man up and take one for the team and teach me.

It was only one game, but I figured it was just kissing, so it can't be too different or difficult after doing it once, right? Or so I thought. I maybe should have practiced a little more. Not too long after, I met this cool, very pretty girl named Sara when I was fourteen.

She was fifteen and a little bit taller than me. She had big blue eyes and long, wavy blond hair, and she had every boy wanting to talk to her. She kind of blew me off at first and said she did not talk to boys younger than she was because they all acted immature.

But after a few days of hard effort, a little persistence, she finally said she would make an exception for me because I acted mature for my age. We met at a park near Mikey's house and started meeting there every day.

One day, we were walking around the park and talking, and Sara said she was thirsty, so we walked to Mikey's house. After we get something to drink, we go into Mikey's room to play Nintendo.

Sara and I started playing a game and picking at each other, and somehow, it led to us wrestling. We ended up sprawled out on the floor of Mikey's room. It turns out she is very ticklish, so I start poking and tickling her sides and ribs, and she is laughing and begging me to stop before she pees on Mikey's floor.

To fend off my tickle attack, she locks her arms around me in a tight bear hug. She is still lying on the floor, but now she has got me pinned down, sort of half draped over her, and we're face-to-face, noses almost touching. She looked at me with this mischievous smile and asked,

"You gonna tickle me if I let you go?"

I laughed, *"Oh, yeah, especially now that you've got me trapped."*

After a few long seconds and a stalemate just looking into each other's eyes, I mustered up the courage to say,

"I won't tickle you if you give me a kiss." She started laughing at me so hard I thought I was going to die with embarrassment.

I was expecting to be released from her bear hug so I could jump off a cliff. But to my surprise, she started kissing me. Before I tell you what happened, let me first say I have always had full-sized lips, which seemed even bigger growing up.

Anyways, we are kissing with her head lying on the floor and with my head over hers. I thought I was doing well because we made out for quite a bit, probably longer than Sara wanted to. When we were finished, I stood up with this big goofy grin, ready to strut like I was the man. I reached out a hand to help Sara up, but her face did not have a smile.

DRINK IN ME

Her face had nothing but saliva on it. Her mouth, chin, nose, and both cheeks were soaked. She rose and, with wide eyes and a little confusion, had to use her shirt like a towel to wipe her face off. And she had a lot to wipe off. I guess the combination of my big lips and inexperience about drowned her.

I walked her back home and there was a heavy kind of silence in the air. Neither one of us said much. I don't think she spoke maybe two words to me while walking home. You can guess I never heard from Sara again. Over time, I became a better kisser, learning to control my big lips and saliva.

You live and learn and you're going to soak at least one face starting out, right? Compared to today's way of dating and how teenagers seem to interact, I almost feel grateful to have grown up in a time before social media and the internet.

There was no Facebook for me, or anyone else, to check and see if someone was telling the truth about their age or anything else. However, we also had the mystery and wonder of what the person looked like because we could not just go online and see their face.

We had to use our imagination and construct an image of what we thought the person might look like from the sound of their voice and their description. You had to talk on the phone first and get to know someone's true personality before you decided to meet them. I can see both pros and cons of having the internet in the palm of your hand.

I guess it's a good thing you can instantly check out someone and see if they are being honest or what they might look like first, but the close interaction you used to experience from phone calls and face-to-face meetings has seemed to disappear.

I feel old saying when I was a teenager from 1993 to 1999, we had to talk and date the "old school" way, as you call it. You had to wait until you met face-to-face before you could swipe left or right. And by that time, you were pretty much stuck for that one date at least.

But, I never decided on dating a girl just because of how wealthy her family was. I never thought about it that way or cared about how rich someone is. Yet, while dating habits evolved with the convenience of technology, there was one thing that remained constant, something much deeper than online profiles or first impressions.

The invisible lines drawn by class and wealth, lines I became all too familiar with as a teenager. When I was fifteen, my family had to move from Hill Street to the projects on Unity Drive, the government housing.

This change would thrust the reality of socioeconomic differences into my daily life, even as I maintained my indifference to wealth. I do not think there is anything wrong with government housing, and I do not believe there is anything wrong with someone who must live there.

I am not a shallow human being who judges people solely on their monetary value. Unfortunately, the school I went to and many of the kids there judged you based on the name of the brand of shoes you had or your clothes.

The only fight at school I ever got into was because of this boy who would not stop picking on me. His name was Ralph, and he was talking shit and messing with me because of my shoes and clothes. He was a little bit bigger than me, like pretty much every other kid was, and one day, he kept on and on. I am not a badass, but after being bullied by Wayne for all those years, no kid at school scared me.

DRINK IN ME

Ralph kept running his mouth all day, and he had two of his little friends laughing and instigating all of it. They would cheer him on and pump Ralph's head up.

He had been daring me to come to the bathroom all day because the bathroom was where boys went to fight without getting caught. I tried to ignore him all day and figured all three might have tried to jump me anyway. Mikey was not there that day to watch my back if they would have tried.

After hearing him talk shit and call me names, near the end of the school day, I had finally had enough.

I raised my hand in class and asked to go to the bathroom, and when I walked by Ralph's desk, I tapped on it. I went to the bathroom, and I waited. Not long after, he and his two cheerleaders came into the bathroom, still pumping his head up.

Ralph walked up to me, got in my face, and asked me what I was going to do, and he shoved me hard. I have never been a person who likes to lip-box someone about what I am going to do, and it takes a lot to piss me off to the point of hitting. But after hearing his shit all day long, and when he shoved me as hard as he did, it was enough to bring out a completely different Timmy.

It was almost a reflex. I instantly slapped the shit out of him, and I grabbed him in a bear hug, picked him up, and slammed him on the bathroom floor. I slammed him on his back, and he let out a loud *"OOOHHH."*

I rose over him while he lay there gasping for air. I raised my fist, and I was going to punch him right in his fuckin' face, but he balled his arms over his head.

48

Suddenly, looking at him, I felt sorry for him. I don't know why I did, hell, he was the one picking on me, but I felt bad for him, so I didn't hit him.

I got up, shoved his head down, and walked out of the bathroom and back to class. He and I became friends after that, and he came to my house a few times to play football with us. But he never picked on me again.

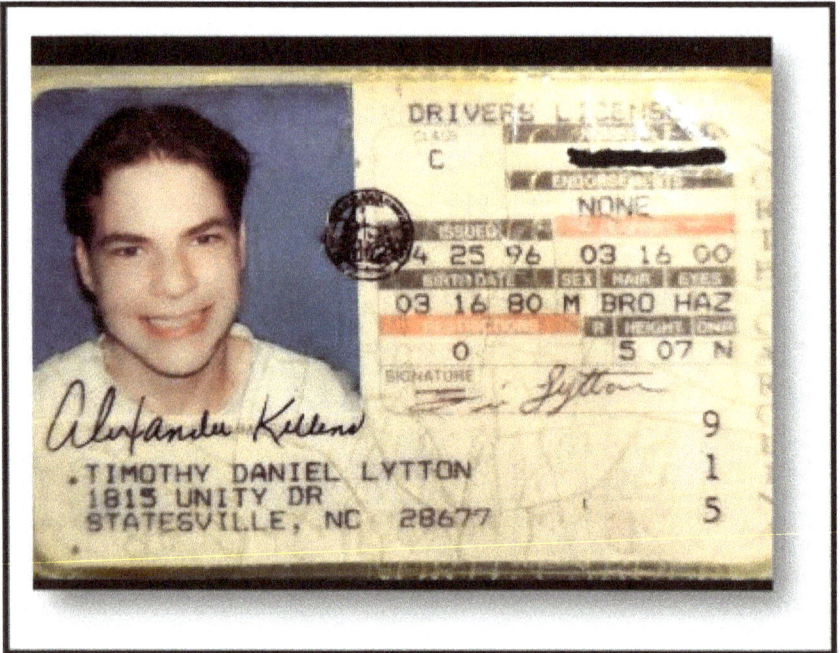

Timmy 16, The day I got my license.

I might have been a little happy.
Just a little!

GLASS #5:

"We accept the love we think we deserve." Stephen Chbosky

Growing up, I was close with all my sisters. Despite their beauty and kind hearts, they were still women, and all had those moments of irritability that could sometimes arise.

My brother and I had to be careful when it was that time of the month; we had to navigate the house like we were walking in a landmine. We could usually tell or guess accurately which sister was on her period because they would have short tempers and give us looks that could kill.

Alternatively, we could ask them a question, and they would bite your head off, but five minutes later, they would apologize with watery eyes. Most of all, they would have one huge stand-alone pimple either in the middle of their chin or right between their eyes.

Whenever we saw those signs, especially if we saw sweatpants, chocolate candy, and pimples, we knew to run the other way.

Despite the lighter moments of sibling intuition, the profound impact my sisters had on my upbringing cannot be overstated. Mary-Jane and Joann deserve a lot of credit for raising me and helping me with many important things. They taught me how to read and write, as well as morals, values, ethics, and the essentials of right and wrong.

DRINK IN ME

Whenever I started dating or going out, my sisters helped me with my hair and clothes. They gave me useful tips and pointers on how to act, what to say, and things most girls like. They would tell me how to treat a lady and would warn me about girls to avoid.

They would point out the good and the bad about a woman and and observe the girls I dated like a mother. My girlfriends would always be nervous about meeting Diane, but I was always nervous about them meeting Mary and Jo.

And like a mother would usually do, Jo and Mary would find something unsatisfactory about every girl I dated. Because of my shyness and lack of smooth talk game, most of the girls I dated either approached me first or were introduced through mutual friends. But no matter how it started, I was always a gentleman.

My sisters made sure of that, by calling me out if I was wrong. Growing up with so many sisters not only taught me to respect and treat my girlfriends the way I'd want my sisters to be treate, but it also enabled me to ask any one of them for advice about the girls I liked.

They not only helped me with advice when I needed it but my sisters would also help me by giving me tips and pointers on how to treat girls and some little things I could do that most girls like.

Like Joann taught me to always ask a lady before you kiss them for the first time. Mary-Jane taught me to never show up on a date empty-handed, to at least have flowers or something. Christie taught me to always tell your lady she is beautiful at least once a day and when she least expects it.

All of it helped me to enjoy and appreciate the natural act of chivalry. Their advice became a quiet mantra for me, especially as I grappled with my shyness and the challenges it brought in expressing myself.

I have always been a shy guy. I dislike being shy by nature and often wish I could be like the guys who seem to have all the confidence to approach any woman and do what I am too shy to do. I am so shy I do not approach anyone unless I have to.

I am not a social butterfly who loves meeting new people. I'm not antisocial or an asshole like many people seem to think before they get to know me. It's because meeting new people is painfully awkward for me, so if I can avoid the uncomfortable feeling, I will.

That is what prevents me from enjoying meeting new people like most normal people. I've probably asked more women on dates by writing them a note with my name and phone number rather than asking them verbally. I know confidence is attractive, but when you sound like a stuttering idiot every time you try to talk to a pretty girl, I'd rather lack confidence.

I have always struggled with verbal communication, particularly when articulating my thoughts or ideas. In contrast, the voice inside my head, which I call "little Timmy," is articulate, intelligent, and can express my thoughts easily and clearly. Strangely enough, I can write out my thoughts better than I can speak to them aloud, which is a source of great frustration and confusion.

How is that even possible? Despite being able to form intelligent thoughts in my head, when I try to verbalize them, I often forget or stumble over my words. I can know something so well in my mind, but if I try to explain what I know, it gets all jumbled up. I have been grappling with this issue for my entire life.

My brother Ricky, on the other hand, has a lot of charisma and charm. He could approach any girl and would always be so smooth and charismatic that he would rarely get rejected. I once saw him making out with two girls at the same time.

DRINK IN ME

One Saturday night, when we were at the skating rink, and it was closing, I was walking around trying to find Ricky. I finally found him outside around the back corner of the building. There was Ricky, taking turns making out with two of the prettiest and most popular girls at their school.

I stood there a minute because, at first, I was not sure I was seeing reality right. I closed my eyes and shook my head, and when I opened them back up, I realized it was true.

Ricky would make out with one of the girls for about a minute, and then would turn his head to the girl on his other side and make out with her for a minute. I could only stand there speechless and admire. I was impressed and a little jealous. I couldn't get one girl to make out with me in a fully lit room, let alone two in a dark corner.

Growing up, Ricky and I were a little different when it came to girls and dating; you would never guess we were brothers.

Ricky would always date as many girls as he could at one time. I have always been the complete opposite. I don't mind dating one girl at a time. I prefer it that way. I would rather have one gold dollar than four quarters or even ten dimes. While Ricky enjoyed the excitement of multiple flings, my slower, more deliberate approach often led to misunderstandings in my relationships.

I have a lot of patience, and something embarrassing is that I have been called "slow" by two girlfriends. Not slow in the head, but slow to put the moves on them. Once as a teenager and another in my thirties. I am not the type who likes to try and pressure a girl. There is nothing wrong with me. I am a regular man, so I am ready whenever. I try to be a gentleman as much as possible, and when it comes to intimacy, the woman ultimately dictates the speed.

My respectful approach shaped my dating experiences, leading to a significant relationship when I was sixteen. I started dating a girl named Rebecca. She was a Libra and had blond hair, blue eyes, fair skin, and a nice butt. We were the same age and had dated for almost a year. Mikey was dating her friend, a girl named Tisha, and on the night I lost my virginity, Rebecca was spending the night with Tisha.

Mikey and I planned to go and hang out with them and Mikey's older brother, Bernie, was supposed to give us a ride, but it started snowing, and it would be a bad winter storm. As North Carolina is not used to big snowstorms, people here are scared to drive in the snow, so Mikey and I had to brave the snowstorm and walk across town. We were freezing and we kept reminding ourselves why we were walking so far.

Of course, we were both hoping to have sex. Mikey had already had sex before, but I had not, so I was extremely nervous but determined. It took Mikey and I a few hours to make it there.

I wore a thick Houston Oilers pullover jacket with a zipper at the neckline, but it did not have a hood, and I had nothing to cover my head. It was so cold, and it was like a blizzard. Mikey and I were not prepared for the cold and the amount of snow. Our toes, fingers, nose, and ears were all so cold they started hurting badly and going numb.

But we were on a mission, and there have been many men who sacrificed pain and endured rough conditions for that magical wonder that had some power that kept us steadily walking nonstop until we got there. We finally made it to Tisha's house late that afternoon, and by the time night came, so much snow had fallen, no one could drive anywhere, so we had to stay the night. Mikey and I were supposed to sleep in the living room, and Tisha and Rebecca were both sleeping in Tisha's room, but the girls told us to sneak down to Tisha's room when everyone else was asleep.

DRINK IN ME

We obeyed and waited until everyone was asleep before heading to Tisha's room. There, Mikey and Tisha were on Tisha's bed making out, and Rebecca and I were on the floor at the foot of the bed. We had the radio playing and were lost in our separate worlds, not paying much attention to what they were doing. Rebecca and I were both virgins, so you can guess things did not go smoothly or even ideally.

We were both nervous and a little hesitant, or at least I was, because we made out and were rubbing on each other for a long time, too long I think. I had never even tried to put a condom on up until this point. So, I pulled the condom out, and she said, *"Oh, let me do it for you."*

Her tone was more exciting than seductive as if she wanted to see if she could do it. I think she was the type of person who always wanted to try everything out of curiosity. Of course, I did not protest and happily handed her the condom with a smile. She takes the condom out of the wrapper and slowly tries to put it on me, but she has it the wrong way, and it will not roll down.

She tries a couple of times to roll it down before realizing she needs to flip it over, so she flips it around and starts to put it on the right way. The bedroom is mostly dark except for the soft glow from a small fish tank on the other side.

For this reason, she is on her knees beside me and leaning over me with her face extremely close so she can see what she is doing. She was holding me with one hand and was focused on what she was doing. She didn't realize how tight of a Kung-Fu grip she had around me, and as she started to roll the condom down the right way with the other hand, I couldn't help it, and I lost control, tensing up with a little body jerk and said, *"Ah."* She immediately pulls the condom back off and lets go of me, asking,

"Did I hurt you?"

At the same time, I shot off like a rocket. She said, "Wow," with surprise as she instinctively tried to pull her face back but her face was just too close, and the first little bit was just too fast, and a small amount landed on her cheek, right below her eye.

There was no warning for me either. She froze with one eye squeezed shut and her hands held up beside her face in the "What do I do" pose. I quickly grabbed my shirt beside me and handed it to her. I was nervously anticipating her reaction and I felt so guilty and embarrassed at the same time. I wanted to run and hide, but luckily, she was cool and did not get mad at me.

She went to the bathroom to wash her face, and I apologized and told her to give me about 30-45 minutes before we could try again.

It was later that night when we got everything to go right. We ended up laughing about it later, and of course, she would joke and tease me a few times. But hey, you live and learn, and you're going to shoot at least one face starting out, right?

I have no choice but to try and laugh and make light of my "not so smooth" past. But it was so painfully embarrassing back then, and I thought it was the end of the world. I have never been cool or smooth like Ricky, and I gave up trying to be a long time ago. Everybody wants to be cool and suave, and I am no different.

But whenever I did try to be a cool guy, it only made things worse, and I would end up looking even more foolish. I had to find a way to be happy and content in my shy awkwardness and learn how to accept myself for me. But even as I embraced my unique self, away from the pressures of appearing cool, I still faced challenges in interpreting a woman's subtle romantic signals, or when someone is flirting with me in any way.

DRINK IN ME

I am clueless when it comes to noticing signs a girl might be interested in me. All my sisters are pretty, and growing up, they would get hit on and asked out a lot, and I would hear them sitting around and talking about how creepy some guy is, how some other guys will not leave them alone, or about some guy's corny one-liner.

My brain assumes that if a woman is friendly and smiles at you, my default thinking has always been that's it. Even if the girl were interested and hoping I would hit on her or flirt with her, I would usually assume she was being nice and try not to bother her or be creepy by trying to get a phone number.Especially if she is pretty, I presume she gets hit on all the time, and I don't want to be just another annoying dude. I mean, how is a guy supposed to know if you want them to hit on you or if you are being nice?

From what I have learned about women in my life, the same woman will give you a different answer to that question each day. Women can be complicated. A lot of them are so same different at different same time. Navigating the complexities of understanding women's signals and hints left me cautious and confused.

Yet a shift in my life brought new experiences and a new relationship that would teach me a very cold and painful lesson. As a teenager, I became a little more self-conscious about my appearance and I would try to dress as nicely as possible. Often, I would be mistaken for a rich boy or wealthy prep, all because I combed my hair and tried to wear clean collared shirts when I could. When I was 17 years old, I got a job as a bag boy at a grocery store close to my house.

Well, the assistant manager was this 19-year-old girl who was extremely attractive. She looked, smelled, and acted like she came from money or the other side of the tracks I was not accustomed to. She was short and petite but had a shapely body.

She had very short blond hair, which I am not a fan of, but her face was pretty enough that she could pull it off. She had blue eyes and a proud and confident personality. I had only been working there a week or two, not long at all. One day, as I was bagging groceries and doing my job, the hot assistant manager started talking to me and asking simple questions such as, do I like my job?

What school did I go to? How are things going? Type of small talk. I am a total dork because I remember at first thinking she was nice but a bit nosy for asking me twenty million questions. I know, I know, I am a dumbass, and looking back, I can see and understand what all her questions and small talk were for. Like I said, I am a complete "Water Boy" when it comes to someone flirting with me.

Later that day, the pretty assistant manager walked by me and said,

"Two uh? I'll take two any day." And she walked off laughing. So, I smiled and gave her a fake little laugh because she was my boss and hot as hell. But I had no idea what the hell she was talking about. I was lost, like in the middle of the woods lost, and started thinking of a thousand possibilities of what this hot and now weird chick was talking about.

She stood at the manager's office window, staring at me with this lovely, playful smile that should have been fun and flirtatious to any normal and smart person. But to a shy, humble, and modest Pisces who is a clueless dumbass, it sent me running to the bathroom.

I washed my hands and splashed water on my face as if it would help splash some sense into my head. I turned sideways to get the paper towel, and something on the back of my uniform vest caught my eye. It was a bright orange "Two for One" sticker dot the store used to mark the "Two for One" sales. I must have accidentally rubbed a product and gotten it stuck on me.

I peeled it off and stared at it as my mind turned gears, putting 2 plus 2 together. It took a few more seconds before the proverbial light bulb lit up brightly in my head, and I thought to myself, "Oh shit, I think she meant two of me?" I am slow to catch on sometimes, but I now had a grin from ear to ear as I fixed my hair in the mirror.

I tightened up, straightened my clothes, and walked out of the bathroom looking crazy with what people call a "Shit Eating Grin" on my face, my heart pounding in a mix of embarrassment and excitement. I was a 17-year-old junior who was not used to hot girls hitting on me. She was a 19-year-old college girl who could have any guy she talked to. Yeah, I might have been strutting and smiling a little bit... Ok, a lot! The next few days were terrific!

We spent our work shifts flirting, and she even offered to give me rides home after work. She drove a nice brand-new sports car, which she said was her graduation gift. After getting into her brand new car, I was too embarrassed to let her see where I lived, so I had her drop me off at Mikey's house. Before I got out of the car, she asked me if I wanted to go on a date with her the following weekend. I said yes but told her I was the guy so I would take her out. She said OK.

Whenever she gave me a ride, we would stop by the park and sit in the car and talk, which would lead to making out, and heavy feeling. And after an hour or two, when we were both so worked up, she would give me a ride to Mikey's house. The closer and closer we got to Saturday, the more intense and passionate the flirting would be and the more intimate the make-out sessions would get. So, Friday night, when she gave me a ride from work and stopped at the park, we were going at it hot and heavy, kissing and touching everywhere. I am in the passenger seat with the backrest laid down, and she is sitting on top of me.

I am a guy, so I can only take so much pressure before I start hurting badly. We were going at the hot and heavy for so long I tapped out. Of course, my fingers were helping her, so I knew at least she was not going to have a very severe case of some bad blue balls.

I said, *"Hey, look, Please, I need to get home. If I stay here any longer, I won't be able to walk tomorrow for our date."* She stopped kissing my neck and sat up, looked at me with a playful smile, and with a matter-of-fact-like tone said,

"Well, we can't let that happen now, can we?" She started to get off of me, but instead of slipping back over to the driver's seat, she knelt in front of me and unbuttoned and unzipped my fly. It was my first oral experience, and what she did next would be much better felt than described.

A combination of my sexual inexperience, the prolonged excitement, plus just the sheer intensity of the pleasure I felt meant it was like two minutes later, and I had my arms wrapped around her head in an overly sensitive blast of pure euphoric pleasure and my breath came out in deep, satisfied puffs as we were on the road and my face could not stop smiling.

I felt so wonderful and happy that I figured surely, after the past week with all the flirting, kissing, rubbing, and now this, it would be okay for "Miss Wonder Mouth" to take me to my house on Unity drive.

She pulls into my driveway and with very wide eyes and blank stare does not say a word. The house, or unit as it was called, was a small brick, poor-looking home. The windows had these dull plain white shades. There was dirt and a few patches of grass for a yard, but no bushes or flowers.I leaned over to kiss her goodnight, and all she would offer was a cheek. I said,

"I'll see you tomorrow evening," As casual as I could sound in hopes of breaking her fixed daze. I got out of the car.

She slowly nodded her head yes and drove off. The next day, Saturday, she didn't call me all day and totally ghosted me. So, the next day, Sunday, I borrowed Joann's car, and I went to her big, fancy, rich house right beside the country club. I remembered the name of the road she lived on from all our conversations. She would brag about it so much it wasn't hard to remember.

I drove down the road slowly until I saw her little sports car parked in front of this gigantic two-story brick home. The house was beautiful and by far the biggest I had ever seen in person. The front lawn was enormous; the grass had a checkerboard pattern, and the bushes and gardens were well-kept. There was a big black metal gate that was closed but not locked.

I found myself holding my breath unconsciously as I walked the paved pathway up to a short flight of steps and a gigantic oak door that had to be at least 15 feet tall, with some decorative design carved in it. I rang the doorbell, and her little sister came to the door. I recognized her little sister from school and one of my classes.

"You're looking for my sister, right?" she asked, smiling shyly.

"Yes... Please" I replied, chuckling uncomfortably.

"Hmm..." she murmured while slowly, looking me over with this mysterious smile in her eyes. *"Alright, wait a sec,"* she said finally, leaving the door slightly ajar as she sprang into the room.

The view inside the slightly open door was breathtaking. The double circular staircases, plush rugs, and antique chandelier, it was a little too intimidating, so I forced myself to return my gaze to the garden. It wasn't long before I could pick up the soft, muffled footsteps of someone wearing socks and approaching the door.

They were careful, deliberate, and rhythmic in their approach; and could only belong to someone I knew already. I turned just in time to see her reach the door and fold her hands across her chest and the forced smile I was bringing up froze on my face. She had the coldest, meanest, expression I'd ever seen, and with a really annoyed tone of voice, she said,

"Can I help you?" I thought Ouch, I said,

"Our date yesterday, you stood me up." She smirked her lips and looked me up and down slowly and deliberately,

"Well, this just isn't going to work between us. I made a big mistake." Her words hit me like a punch to my gut, and I was stunned for a few seconds. I could still see the shadow her younger sister's body was making standing behind her. I wanted to ask her whether Friday night was a mistake or not. But for some reason, I could not force those words out.

I looked right into her eyes for a very long, awkward moment and replied, "I'm sorry to bother you then." and walked away. I am not going to lie; that hurt like hell, and having to swallow it while she stood there and watched me walk away stung and burned like acid on my feelings. I actually felt less than human. I had always thought if you like someone, it's because of who they are and how they treat you and nothing else matters. I found out the hard way: not everyone feels the same. But in the end, it spoke of her character more than it did mine.

To judge someone solely on their monetary wealth is just as shallow, ignorant, and hurtful as judging someone solely on race, religion, gender, or any other reason. Unfortunately, it would not be the last time I would be judged and mistreated for being poor.

Tim 18,   Mikey 18,   1998.

GLASS #6:

"Eighteen is a magic birthday that signifies the end of childhood and the beginning of adulthood." - Debasish Mridha

Year 18 was meant to be an exciting and significant year for me. Graduating from high school, becoming an adult, and contemplating the future. Initially, I considered joining the army to have them pay for my college education. However, the year eighteen will always be remembered for all the wrong reasons.

In 1998, I was eighteen years old and had just started my senior year in high school. I was your typical eighteen-year-old guy. I liked hanging out with friends and family, watching movies, playing basketball or football behind Mikey's house, or going to the mall and walking around or just sitting around smoking weed.

One of our favorite things to do was smoke weed and play Nintendo games that four people could play together; no matter what we were doing, we were sure to be stoned. I was a huge pothead back then. Hell, one of the main reasons I took on a part-time job delivering pizzas was for weed money.

I worked after school and on the weekends at a small pizza place called "Turn 4 Pizza," which had a racing theme. The best part of the job was that most of my coworkers were close friends.

DRINK IN ME

I worked alongside Mikey, Terry, their older brother Bernie, and their younger brother Brian. We all got along great since we all grew up together. Bernie was a manager, and he generously allowed me to use his car for pizza deliveries since I didn't have a vehicle of my own.

It was a blast getting high, going to work with friends, and having the freedom to whip up pizza, wings, salad whenever the munchies struck.

I met Shawna in late September of '98. She called my house, looking for Terry, Mikey's brother. You see, Mikey and Terry often used my family's number as their own since they practically lived at my house. She called a few times, trying to reach him. The funny thing was, every time she called, Terry wasn't around, and I happened to be the one answering the phone.

So, I gave her our work number at Turn 4 Pizza, and I guess she finally got a hold of him because the next time I saw Terry, I told him about Shawna calling, and he said,

"Yeah, I talked to her. She doesn't seem to be my type."

I shrugged it off, thinking I would not hear anything more about Shawna. But the next day, or maybe the day after, my home phone rang, and it was Shawna.

I said, *"Sorry, Terry isn't around."*

She said, *"I'm not calling for Terry; I'm calling to talk to you. Your voice caught my attention, and I figured it wouldn't hurt to have a chat with you."*

That caught me by surprise, and I said, *"Oh...well... Thank you. I like the sound of your voice, too."*

"Well, Tim, tell me something interesting about yourself..."

"Hmm, let's see... I am 18, a senior at Statesville High School, I deliver pizza part-time, oh, and I'm just learning to play the guitar, and I'm a Pisces. What about you?"

"Well, I'm Shawna, of course you know that. I'm 16 years old, and I'm a sophomore at West Iredell High School. I like to draw and play volleyball.. Oh, and I'm a Virgo."

And just like that, we started talking to each other every day for the next week or two, getting to know each other better. I found myself able to talk to Shawna for hours at a time without getting bored or restless. After about two weeks, Shawna called me and said,

*"Come and meet me Tomorrow after church."**"I would love to meet up, too, but I don't do the church thing. I would feel so uncomfortably out of place,"* I replied sadly.

"Oh, it's just, you know, we haven't had a chance to meet in person yet and see what each other looks like. And I really want to see you," she said seriously.

"Do I have to dress in my Sunday best, and meet a lot of people?"

She chuckled, *"No, no! You don't have to come to church service. It's a youth program that my brother and I have to attend every week because it looks good on the family. Just come around 7 p.m., when the program ends. I can walk away from my brother so that you and I can talk for a few minutes."*

"Oh, alright. I can do that."

For the next couple minutes, the call lasted; I was grinning smugly from ear to ear, hyped up by her excitement about meeting me the next day.

I was at the church earlier than 7 pm, but it wasn't that hard to wait. I had smoked a whole joint by myself on the way to the church because I was so anxious and nervous at the same time.

DRINK IN ME

I was as high as any Apollo mission. For one, the church had beautiful surroundings with trees and all of that, so it was easy for me to lose myself gazing off at the amazing setting sun, which seemed to be disappearing into thin smoke-like clouds.

Eventually, the huge front doors of the church were thrown open, and I could see people pouring out of the building like they had been dying for a chance to get out and calling friends as they went.

Blue jean overalls and a red and black striped flannel shirt I muttered repeatedly to myself as my eyes scanned the crowd of people trooping out of the building. It was dizzying in a way, watching so many people closely at once, in their array of different colors and styles of fashion.

Soon, repeating what Shawna had told me she would be wearing felt like chanting a magical prayer to make her appear at once. I started thinking about how wonderful it was getting to know her the past few weeks. How we can talk about anything and everything with such ease I would find myself not wanting the conversation to end when we would talk on the phone. It was something new for me.

I had never been attracted to someone's personality as much as hers. I drew a sharp breath just as my anxiety was creeping in. My stoned brain started wandering in all different directions.

I wondered how good or attractive any woman can be in overalls and a flannel shirt. I had never seen a supermodel wearing that outfit. I started wondering if she would look like a farm girl who played with goats.

When we talked, she told me about her farm animals and how she loved to play with her goats.

I was beginning to freak myself out, and my feet started to turn toward the parking lot. I thought about running to the car.

I shook my head hard from side to side as if to shake off my paranoid thoughts, trying not to let the weed high get the better of me.

Just as I was about to bolt, I saw her. My eyes opened wide with amazement, and I bit my lip to hold back the sheepish grin that was threatening to spread across my face.

Keeping a dedicated eye on her, I started picking my way through the crowd to her. She was beautiful. I knew how incredible and attractive her personality was, but my stoned brain was not prepared to look at such beauty.

She was walking beside her brother. Shawna had told me about her brother once when we talked on the phone. I recognized him now, walking beside her with a slight stoop and a quiet manner about him. He had short blonde hair and a calm, almost somber expression.

Whenever Shawna spoke about her brother, it was with so much fondness that I knew he meant a lot to her. He also seemed like a nice person to me.

I hate subsequently after I started dating Shawna, I would meet her brother only once, and we didn't say much, so I didn't get to have a relationship with him and only knew a little about him from what Shawna told me. Suddenly, I saw her face light up; she had seen me.

I noticed her nudge her brother slightly, and he looked at me. In that brief split second, I held his gaze, and we shared a greeting ever so slightly; he nodded to his sister, and she fell out of step with him. Shawna walks up to me, and I am speechless.

DRINK IN ME

She was about 5'5 and 120 lbs. Her smooth blond hair was parted in the middle and laid flat and a little past her chin on each side of her face. She has a soft, smooth complexion and big, round, light blue eyes.

"Pleasure to meet you my lady," I bowed, presenting a small bunch of colorful flowers I'd picked up at the store on my way. She raised one hand to cover her mouth and giggled sweetly.

"The pleasure is mine, my lord," she chimed and mock-bowed like she was wearing a huge gown as she accepted the flowers.

The fact that she was in literal jean overalls made the entire scene look weirder and funnier, and it was me who had trouble trying not to laugh too awkwardly. I nervously stuck my hands in my pocket and glanced down at my feet so my staring would not be overly obvious.

"They're really pretty," she gushed, feeling the petals delicately one by one.

"Yet they wouldn't hold a candle to you," I replied, lifting my head to look at her and smiling at how beautiful her smile looked. I thought she was beautiful —in a soft, kind, and delicate kind of way. She blushed delicately, smiling widely at me with a mouth full of braces.

"Your braces are cute."

She smiled even more, but this time, it was she who looked away.

"So, no work today?" she asked when she turned to look at me again, a shy smile played on her lips.

"I took the night off."

"What about people wanting to eat pizza tonight?" she teased.

70

"I guess those people will have to eat DiGiorno; I had a very special date," I said with a wink. Shawna's smile widened as her cheeks flushed red.

"Oh, really? She's a lucky girl."

"Not nearly as lucky as I am," I replied, turning to walk slowly towards the direction her brother had gone. Shawna took my hand and said,

"Come, follow me."

And we hurried around to the back of the church, where there was a small corridor that had an outside stairwell.

We stopped under the stairwell, and we stood there for a minute and looked around as if expecting to see someone following us or as if we were being chased, but there was no one. I turned to look at her face, which was even closer to mine now.

I could see her flawless complexion and her captivating eyes for all their glory. She was even more beautiful the closer I got, and we stared into each other's eyes, not saying a word for what seemed like hours.

She was still holding my hand, so I took my free hand, and I grabbed her other hand, and gently pulled her closer to me to where our noses almost touched. I felt a burning desire to kiss her soft-looking lips, and I started to lower my face to hers, but then I stopped and hesitated, with our lips almost touching.

Her eyes were closed in anticipation, but I remembered being a gentleman and always asking a lady before you kiss her for the first time. I would always take heed of the advice and tips my sisters would give me about how to treat a lady, and at least the ladies I dated seemed to appreciate it.

DRINK IN ME

"Can I kiss you?" I asked Shawna with my voice soft and barely above a whisper.

"Yes, please...!" She responded.

I slowly lowered my head until my lips met hers. At that moment, I felt an indescribable explosion of pure bliss and absolute peace and joy in my heart. A feeling I had never felt washed over me, and I could not help but lose the world around me as if only she and I existed. Our kiss ended as softly as it began, and with a weak and breathless voice, she said,

"I wish you could have walked me home, so we'd have more time to talk. There's something I want to tell you, but I don't have time right now."

"Ok...? Some other day then," I replied casually.

"I really have to go before my dad comes looking for me; if he finds me back here wit...." She stopped, her eyes widening in shock. Her dad had come around the corner of the church and noticed her and I standing there talking, and he just yelled her name out loudly, cutting her off mid-speech as he stomped his way toward us.

"Calm down..." I muttered, flustered at why she was so scared and why her dad looked so angry.

"You don't understand," she said in a faint voice as her dad walked up.

"What the hell....?" He growled, eyeing me coldly as he snatched his daughter's hand up and dragged her away from me.

I stared right back at him, frowning confusedly and feeling slightly miffed. Finally, he looked away and moved his grip from Shawna's palm to the point up her arm right below her shoulder.

I was still standing and watching them leave when Shawna turned back for a second to blow a kiss at me. I smiled and caught it while she looked away just as quickly. From that moment on, we couldn't get enough of each other.

We made every effort to spend as much time together as possible, seizing any opportunity for Shawna to escape what she often called her prison-like home. She confided in me about her parents' excessive control and how they imposed strict limitations on her dating life. I understood her struggle because when Wayne lived with us, my sisters weren't allowed to date, and none of us could have friends.

She had her phone line, but her dad would always come up with any reason to take it from her, and she could never do anything right, it seemed. Usually, I would drive to her house to pick her up, but she preferred to meet me outside because Shawna had no desire for me to meet her asshole dad or her mom, and I was ok with that.

Our favorite hangout spot was usually my sister Mary-Jane's house. Mary worked the evening shift as a Certified Nursing Assistant (C.N.A) at a nursing home, and she generously allowed Shawna and me to spend our time there playing video games and watching movies. Other times, we would ride around town or spend time together casually at the park and talk. We could talk about anything and everything and would talk for hours, just enjoying ourselves.

Every time we talked, somehow, it always circled back to school, work, and family, and Shawna would tell me how much she hated being at home. She would tell me how she was a slave and did whatever hard labor she was made to. The second time we met was at my sister Mary-Jane's apartment, and I remember the wistful longing in her eyes as she fingered the curtains, wallpaper, and even Mary's stereo set.

DRINK IN ME

"I wish I lived here," she said finally after like five minutes of silence while she just stopped and fingered random things in the house.

"Shawna, it's just a regular apartment," I said quietly and a bit concerned.

When she turned to look at me, there was so much intensity in her eyes as she repeated that she wished she lived here with her brother, except it would be in a very far place where neither her mom nor dad could find her.

Inwardly, I dismissed it as the usual longing we all must be away from our parents, but something about her tone nagged at me all day after I saw her off at home. I sometimes wish I had noticed the signs; all was not so cool at Shawna's house earlier than when I did. But what could I have done?

I had grown up under Wayne's abusive watch, and the authorities were never able to make him stop, so much so we had to start calling my grandma to help. About a month into our relationship, I picked her up one night, and she raced out of the house the moment she caught a glimpse of me from her bedroom window and into my arms, crying profusely.

She had caught her brother trying to commit suicide by tying a noose around his neck, and it was the first time he had attempted. Unfortunately, it would not be the last.

I wondered just how bad things inside Shawna's home were for her brother to do that. Later that day, sitting in Mary-Jane's apartment, Shawna's sobs quietened to occasional sighs, and with my arm around her, she told me she and her brother were adopted.

It made sense, finally, how it seemed Shawna and her brother were a far cry from what their parents looked like, and I shivered to think what Wayne might have done to Ricky and me if we were his adopted kids instead.

There were more signs every time I picked her up: bruises on her arms and neck, a sharp gasp and wince when I playfully tickled her or put my hand anywhere near her torso, and one time, I saw a large red welt on the side of her ribs.

Her explanations were just as obvious to me, too—a sideways glance and awkward attempt to hurriedly explain how she had tripped while doing these stunts a girl dared her to do at the gym or how her pet goats liked to play rough sometimes.

That was her favorite reason. She loved her goats and would tell me how much she loved spending time with them. The love for her animals was about the only joy she had in that prison of a home.

I knew she was not telling the truth about the bruises and marks, but what good would it do to make her tell me the truth? I think the abuse was an unspoken bond between us, and it even brought our hearts even closer together.

I knew exactly how she felt and the pain and shame of being abused. So, when I would hold her and comfort her, I would wrap my arms tight as I wish someone would have done for me whenever Wayne was abusing me.

Sometimes, when I'd hang out with Ricky and Mikey late into the night after I closed from work, we'd have these conversations about girls. Ricky would tell me how it made you "feel less than a man" if your girl was cheating on you with another man, and I'd wonder to myself, how one could feel less than a man.

But now it made sense. When Shawna would make those vague cover-ups for why she got those bruises on her, I'd see the raw pain in her eyes simmering behind a thin film of moisture, and I swear it couldn't have hurt more if I was kicked in the balls just then.

DRINK IN ME

I'd get a literal tearing pain in my chest and have to clench my fists just so it wouldn't be obvious my hands were unsteady.

From then until I got home and the next day and the day after that, I would mope around feeling like the world's biggest loser because what kind of man stood by and watched his girlfriend get beaten up?

I felt so small, like a pathetic little wimp, and for the second time since I'd known Wayne, I longed for a reason to get into a fight with someone, Shawna's Dad. Only this time it was a more insane, more primal desire to do some real damage.

It was the only thing that got me up and fighting for our relationship, and that made me kiss those bruises and soothe the swells away, the hope that one day I'd make it right to her.

When I would see her home for the night, she would cling to me so tightly that I wondered if I was not a coward for being the one to lead her to the one place that she hated to be in. But I understood she did not want to talk about all of that, at least not yet.

So, I would mask what I felt and try to talk about something else that wasn't triggering. Shawna and I were supposed to hang out and meet at a Halloween party, but when it was time, she wasn't there, and since then I'd been anxiously waiting to hear from her for a few days.

I tried to call her house a few times, but her mom or dad would answer and give me the nastiest attitude, and they would say Shawna's busy or she's not at home, so I took the hint and stopped trying. I would wait for Shawna to call me. I was concerned about her, but what could I do?

Finally, after almost a week, Shawna called one night when I was closing work. She wanted to see me and make up for not being available for our date on Halloween night. I had a ton of questions, but I promised her I would be there in ten minutes, tops. I closed Turn 4 Pizza quickly, got Bernie's car keys from him, and in no time, I was heading towards Shawna. She wore a loose shirt and jeans, black sunglasses, and a headband that had rabbit ears over her hair.

"What are you doing?" I teased and laughed, surprised at how insanely happy I was just to see her as she settled into the passenger seat clumsily, laughing and fastening her seatbelt.

"It's my costume. I'm trying to be the little rabbit man from Alice in Wonderland," she piped breathlessly and leaned in to kiss me.

"I never did read that book, but I'm sure the little rabbit didn't wear a pair of sunglasses," I replied when she let me go.

"That's because he's not as cool as I am," she bragged, wriggling off me and back to the passenger seat. *"And, of course, the little rabbit needed to put on spectacles when he read from his little note for what the Queen wanted,"* she added triumphantly.

"We're past Halloween, silly." I laughed, and we drove to Mary-Jane's apartment, talking in easy, low tunes all the way.

"There you go," I announced cheerfully as soon as we had gotten safely indoors.

I felt for the switch and flicked it on, and for a moment, I just watched Shawna stand in the doorway, breathing in the air and admiring the lights and décor like she was seeing them for the first time again. She looked beautiful, almost aglow, except for those ridiculously huge sunglasses.

DRINK IN ME

"I think you could play the part of the white rabbit with very little costume, though," I teased, gently tugging the little band that she had used to hold her hair up in a bun so that it fell loose.

"You're so beautiful, Shawna," I whispered and kissed her gently on the lips.

"And you just look insanely cute with those silly rabbit ears," I laughed, stepping back to look at her and feeling like the luckiest person in the world.

"Here, let's get this off," I whispered and raised my hand to take the glasses off her face.

"No. Stop." She mumbled while blocking my hands and pulling her face away. That was definitely unexpected, I decided, peering curiously at her in the soft light of Mary's living room. She appeared shy, scared even, and I was now suspecting the sunglasses were not merely a costume.

"Come over here," I whispered, leading her onto the only couch in the room, a triple sofa kind of thing, and letting her sit on my lap.

I reached for the shades again. This time, she did not try to stop me, and slowly, I took off the glasses to reveal an almost swollen-shut black eye.

"Ho-lee shit!" My heart sank all the way to my knees, and I suddenly felt a chill run through me like I might be coming down with a fever.

"What happened to you, Shawna?" I whispered, doing my best to keep my frustration and anger out of my voice and cupping her face in my hands so I would get her other full eye up to look at me.

She would not look at me, though, deciding to focus on a spot somewhere above my pants beltline, yet I could see the shame and embarrassment in her one-and-a-half eyes.

"Shawna... what happened?" I asked softly again when she would not answer.

"Umm... you know it's just really nothing."

"I still want to know," I replied after a long pause, but no more explanations were forthcoming.

"It was during volleyball practice at the gym, and this girl elbowed me," she replied a little too smoothly, keeping her one good eye looking down. I just nodded silently and hugged her tighter. A kind of brooding silence hung between us, and I wondered just what had happened on the Halloween night that was supposed to be our date.

"You know you can tell me anything, right?" I whispered, kneading my hands in her hair. She did not say anything, only hugged me tighter. *"If it was a hit during volleyball practice, why were you hiding it in the first place?"*

I asked in a much lighter tone. I had calmed myself down enough to make light of the matter while I was with her. Of course, I knew she was lying, maybe because she thought I would freak out and stop wanting to see her, I reasoned. Either way, I'd promised I wouldn't make her tell me if she didn't want to. I'd let her do it when she felt it was right. I would just go and nurture my thoughts of righting the wrongs the bastard was doing to her when I was by myself again.

"Because..., I felt you'd think I was ugly."

That broke my heart—the honesty and vulnerability in her tone.

"Look at me Shawna," I whispered urgently, cupping her cheeks with my hands so her eye had to look into mine. *"You can have a black eye, no teeth, a bald head, and peg leg and still be one of the prettiest girls ever to me."*

She held my gaze for the longest time, as if to gauge the honesty in my words, and then just kissed me.

As far as kisses go, it was one of the most intense and most passionate kisses we ever shared. After that, we just sat there silently for a long time.

She was still on my lap with her arms wrapped around my neck and her head lying on my shoulder. I held her with one arm around her waist, and my other hand rubbed her head and hair lightly. Neither of us said a word for almost an hour, which was so unlike Shawna, so I knew something was deeply wrong.

"Hey, forget about all the sad drama while you're here with me. For the short amount of time that we are together, milady, you are royalty. There's no room for frowns in Mary-Jane's Neat Freak Kingdom," I said while offering her a warm smile, hoping to brighten her mood.

She paused for a long moment, looking at me hard and deep with her one good eye as if trying to find the strength to join me. Finally, she returned the smile and said,

"You're right, my lord, Sir Tim. Please forgive me."

"That's the spirit," I grinned, rising to my feet and playfully puffing out my chest.

Striking a comical pose, I declared, "When you are here, you're Princess Lady Shawna, and I'm your loyal, trusted knight in cotton armor, Sir Tim. It's my duty not only to protect the princess but also to ensure her heavenly face wears nothing but a smile."

"Are you going to protect me, Sir Knight?" Shawna played along, giving a mock curtsy.

"Indeed, Your Highness. I will guard you with my very own life if needed. So beware, the kingdom has many dangers, like the little gang of mischievous sock thieves. Those tiny golems living in people's dryers who love snatching one sock at a time. They are ruthless culprits who will stop at nothing to cause chaos to your laundry and are responsible for that mysterious one missing sock that can't be explained." I added in my best attempt to be straight-faced, serious, and with a conspiratorial tone and secretive wink.

Shawna looked a little puzzled while her mind was processing my words. She gazed at me with an amused grin for a moment. Then her eyebrows shot up in delight, and she burst into laughter with her one eye open wide.

"So, you mean to tell me that's why I sometimes lose a sock after doing a load of laundry? You're saying there are little golems living in dryers, dedicated to stealing people's socks? And how do I defend against these sock thieves?" she inquired between laughs.

"They have two weaknesses, my lady. Firstly, they are hypnotized by a beautiful woman wearing nothing but socks, unable to look away. Secondly, they cannot resist disco music. When they hear it, they can't help but dance uncontrollably. But fear not, for when you are with me, I shall keep you safe," I proclaimed with a smile while doing my best attempt to dance the 70's classic "rolling arms and pointing upwards" style dance, all while playfully singing, *"Staying alive, staying alive, Oh, Oh, Oh, Oh, staying alive."*

Shawna could not control her laughter and began to laugh so hard that she snorted like a pig. That caused me to laugh at her laughing, which made her laugh and snort even more. Finally, after a long, hard laughing fit, we both calmed down. Shawna leaned in, a playful spark in her eye as she struggled to suppress her laughter and regain a serious demeanor.

DRINK IN ME

"Well, how should I reward you, brave knight?" she asked, her finger tracing a tantalizing path down my chest.

"Ah, I have but one humble request: a gentle kiss from a beautiful princess, wearing only her royal socks," I teased, flashing a charming smile and winking.

"Is that so?" she said, locking her gaze with mine, her smile carrying a hint of mystery. Without saying another word, she turned, walked away, and entered Mary-Jane's bedroom. I stood there, somewhat puzzled, for a moment or two until a soft voice beckoned me from the bedroom.

"Um..., are you coming, Sir Tim?"

I made my way to the bedroom and froze in my tracks just inside the doorway. Shawna stood beside Mary-Jane's queen-size bed, wearing nothing but a confident smirk and a pair of white socks. My eyes widened, taking in the breathtaking sight before me. I was left utterly speechless, my jaw hanging open.

I felt like a cartoon character with oversized eyes and a jaw lying on the floor. Shawna stood elegantly by the bed; her right leg crossed over her left. Her 5'5" frame accentuated her 120-pound form perfectly.

Beauty, they say, is in the eye of the beholder, and at that moment, in time and space, Shawna was beholding all the beauty I could imagine in my 18 years of existence. Shawna finally spoke, breaking my hypnotized trance.

"What kind of princess would I be if I denied a heroic knight his wish?" she remarked, her hands resting on her perfectly shaped hourglass hips.

"As a princess, I do have one small request. The knight can only wear his royal socks if he wants his reward kiss." Her raised eyebrows conveyed her command, and I quickly followed suit and began shedding my clothing and moving closer to her.

I tried my best to be cool, but like always, my attempt at being smooth and undressing while walking ended with me tripping and almost falling as my pants got stuck around my ankles. Shawna chuckled and shook her head, but I was unfazed. By the time I made it to her, I, too, was wearing nothing but a smile and socks.

"I'm delighted to see you smiling again, my lady," I whispered as I wrapped my arms around her, pulling her close.

"Thank you. You truly are my knight," she murmured, her arms encircling my neck.

"Are you sure about this?" I asked, locking eyes with her. She nodded, her voice barely above a whisper.

"I've never been more certain."

"In that case, Your Highness, I believe it's time for that kiss."

I drew nearer, our faces just an inch apart. Shawna closed her eyes in anticipation, and slowly, our lips met in a tender, passionate kiss as we tumbled onto the bed.

Later that night, I parked Bernie's car two blocks away from Shawna's house and killed the lights. She was leaning close enough to me to put her hands around my neck and mess with my hair at the same time. She was telling me something in soft whispers, and I wasn't paying attention, just staring off numbly at the little drops of rain that spattered on the windshield of the car.

I felt the warmest and safest when I was with Shawna. But she did not feel quite that way when she was with me, I thought bitterly.

DRINK IN ME

It'd always hurt whenever I saw any of those hit marks on her body, but today was different. I felt like I had begun to internalize her pain so much that I felt it as a kind of visceral churning in my belly. How much had it hurt? Did she still feel pain now? How could I help? Or what could I do?

When I saw her body and the full extent of the marks and bruises, it made my hands shake and my chest rip in pain. I could not understand how such beauty could be covered in so much hate.

What could Shawna possibly do to make someone want to hurt her so badly? She was sweet, kind and polite. Yet, there were so many bruises, more than I had ever seen on her before, all the way from her shoulder down to her hip on the left side.

Half of her torso body was covered with purple and deep red bruises, as if someone had repeatedly hit or kicked her while she lay on the ground. That coupled with the almost shut black eye and a dozen more other bruises I knew nothing about.

I turned to look at her, smiling a little at something she was saying because it sounded like a joke. There was definitely pain masking behind those eyes, I thought, feeling a deeper pain in my belly.

"Shawna," I breathed, wishing I had something better to say than what I was about to say. She stopped talking and stared up at me with eager anticipation.

"Girl, I'm dumb. Don't get your hopes up," I scoffed. "You know if you're catching a hard time for talking to me or being with me, as much as I care about you, I am not worth all the goat hits or volleyball elbows." I think I looked pathetic cause she was the one holding up my face in her hands and smiling softly at me.

"I think you're worth every damn bit," she whispered. I pursed my lips and fought the tears that welled up in my eyes.

"Besides, my goats have always played rough. But I better be going before someone discovers my brother's coverup," she smiled, winking at me with her one good eye. I smiled back and pulled her in for one last kiss.

It's sad that when I look back, these were the most blissful days of our relationship and romance we'd kindled and nurtured so tenderly. I'd grossly underestimated what lengths her parents were going to go to see we were never a couple and how I would suffer greatly for it. But for the moment, we grew closer until late in December.

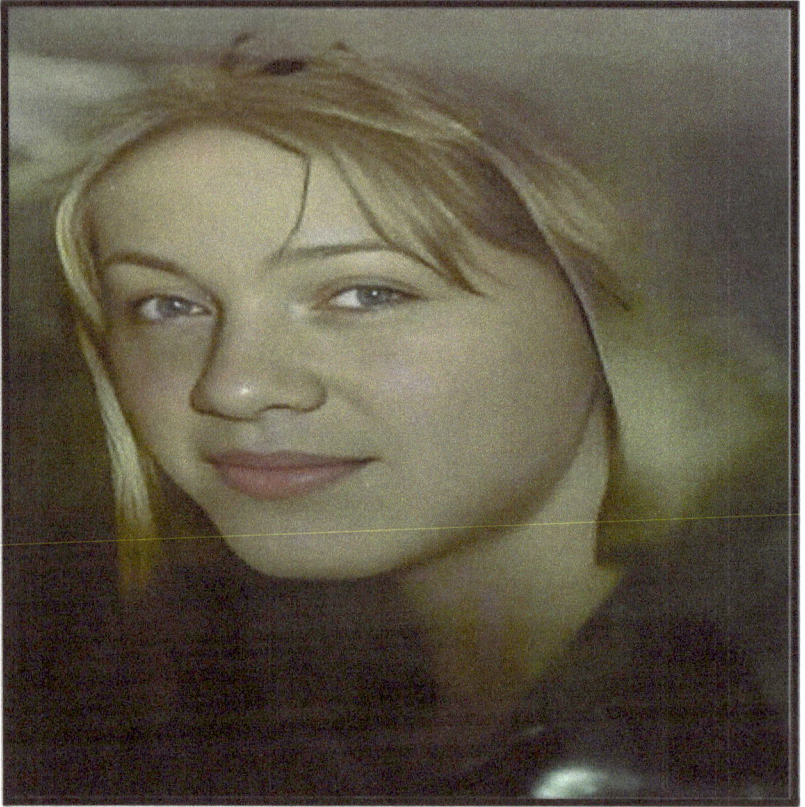

Shawna December, 1998.

GLASS #7:

"Truth is like the sun. You can shut it out for a time, but it ain't going away." - Elvis Presley

I watched people walk in and out of the Iredell County Probation Department with bored, heavy eyelids and a sincere desire to be doing anything else but this. I hissed impatiently; it'd been a little longer than 30 minutes since Ricky went in and he'd promised it wouldn't take long. It would take forever if all I did was stare at the digital clock on the dashboard of Joann's car.

Ricky had gotten involved with the police on a simple weed charge and, at the time, did not have his license. So, I drove him to meet his probation officer for the first time.

I decided to resign myself, stretching my legs as far as the cramped driver's space of the car would allow, and closed my eyes for a moment as I rested my head on the steering wheel, letting my mind drift to the night before.

With Christmas approaching in just a few days, I decided to give Shawna the present I had picked out for her. A black Onyx ring with a silver band. The lady at the jewelry store told me that black Onyx stone was known for its protective properties and that people wear it to guard against evil and negative energy. I thought it was the perfect gift for Shawna and exactly what she needed with everything she was going through. When she opened the box, her face lit up with joy, and she loved it.

So, I thought I would use the opportunity to ask Shawna to be my girlfriend. But, to my surprise, instead of an enthusiastic response, her smile turned into a confused frown.

"I thought I already was," she said, her tone mixed with hurt and confusion. *"Haven't we been acting like we are?"*

"Well, yes...we are, and... we have been..." I stuttered, caught off-guard, trying to find the right words. Shawna's raised eyebrow and expectant look only added to my nervousness. This moment had played out very differently in my head. I was not prepared for this and was fumbling for an explanation, *"I'm sorry, I... I didn't mean you weren't. I... just wanted to ask you, properly, out of respect. It's what people do...right?"*

"So, we were just friends this whole time, uh?" Shawna asked seriously, her eyebrows furrowing in disbelief.

"No! Well...yes! I mean...you are also my friend..."

Shawna burst into laughter before I could finish. Confused and embarrassed, I couldn't help but shake my head and laugh at how silly I felt sitting there as she giggled uncontrollably.

"Good one, Haha. Real funny..." I said with a smile and a ton of relief as I playfully nodged her with my shoulder.

"I was just messing with you! Of course, I'll be your girlfriend. I've been yours since the first day we met." She slipped the ring onto her finger, still chuckling as she said, *"You're too easy, Tim."*

Lost in the pleasant memory, resting my head on the steering wheel, I must have dozed off when I was woken up to the nagging tap-tapping sound of a person who was desperate to get my attention by rapping on the driver's window of the car.

I raised my head with heavy eyes, hoping I had parked in the right spot, and was ready to explain to whoever the official was that I was waiting for my brother.

"You roll down this damn glass. I need to talk to you," came the high-pitched, raspy tone of the moderately overweight red-faced woman on the other side of the driver's window, muffled by the glass separating us. I recognized the homely butch right away, although I didn't understand what it was, she wanted to speak to me about or how she even knew I was sitting there to start with. She was Shawna's mom.

"You need to roll down this damn window." She was speaking loudly and fast before I had even rolled down the window properly, wagging a finger at me as she went. I stared silently at her for a while with the irritated and confused frown one might have if you had just been rudely awakened from a nap to Karen's unstoppable screech.

"Let me tell you right now, right here, you need to stop calling our home and leave Shawna the fuck alone. You hear me? You're not good enough for Shawna, and she is going to do way better than you ever will or can dream of, and me and her father want to make sure she is not distracted by such a person as.....you," she finished, pausing just before the 'you' to look me over with this disgusting, bitchy look on her face.

I had been watching her yell at me, all the while not speaking, letting myself get carried away by what I considered a spectacle of inflating red cheeks and a continuously bobbing short blonde ponytail, but that last line kind of inflamed me a bit.

"Is that why Shawna always has those marks and bruises on her body that look like the result of severe beatings? Or.... animal attacks, of course?" I added with a rather cynical expression.

That took her back a bit, and I could see the anger and shame rising in her face. I was going to celebrate with a smug smile, but she recovered quickly enough to shoot me the nastiest look ever and one last burn.

"Just stay the hell away from my fourteen-year-old daughter, you piece of shit trash!" she muttered under her breath before stomping away.

"Ho-ly shit! What?"

That hit me like a ton of bricks in the chest. What the fuck! Shawna was sixteen! Why the hell would she be lying?! I was frozen in disbelief and shock, as my wide eyes could only stare out of the windshield, looking ahead but not focusing on anything. My mind racing in circles trying to find some kind of rational thought. Did I hear Bertha correctly? I felt lightheaded and dizzy, and maybe even a bit nauseous.

I talked to Ricky about meeting Shawna's mom when we were finally on our way home from the Probation Department. He asked if there was a problem. I didn't tell him everything because I didn't want him to worry about me, and not before I had a chance to talk to Shawna to find out for myself what was going on.

The fact that Shawna's mother (Bertha) had gotten to meet me because she worked as a secretary at the Probation Office, and she had recognized Ricky's last name and asked him if he was related to me made me uneasy.

I mulled over what the chances she would influence my brother's probation decisions and stuff to get to me or how much beating Shawna would have to endure this time, and none were light, optimistic thoughts. I also wondered to myself, why now? Shawna and I had been dating for three months, and her parents knew about me from day one when I met her at the church.

Even though I had not officially met them, they still knew all about me and Shawna because I would call her house and pick her up. They could have said something long before this. Why wait until now to say something? I had so many questions and so much confusion. I was waiting eagerly to talk to Shawna, but I guess they were making sure she did not call me.

I had no way to speak to her to find out what was going on and why she would lie to me. I knew our relationship couldn't continue, but I still needed to ask her why and if she knew what trouble it could cause me. At first, I was angry about being lied to, but once I thought about it and had a little time to contemplate things, I realized I could understand the reason behind the lie. I mean, there could only be one reason for the lie. Shawna knew I would not have dated her if she had told me her real age, just like Heather wouldn't have given me a chance when I was twelve and lied to her. But I didn't know if Shawna realized the significance and possible consequences for me.

I was confused, hurt, scared, lost, but most of all, worried and didn't know what to do. I found someone who went to Shawna's school, and I wrote her a letter asking her all the many questions I had. I tried to recall any sign I missed or something that would have given me a reason to question her age. But there was nothing. A huge part of my attraction to Shawna was her intelligence, and she never did anything to cause doubt or make me suspicious. I didn't have time to think about any of it because Shawna's dad found my letter asking her why she would lie to me.

It was a few days later, and my life would get a little messed up.

-===

DRINK IN ME

I am sure we all have these events and life-altering moments in our lives, and no matter how good or bad the event is, you will never forget every detail and moment of that day.

Unfortunately, the main reason for these moments is more than often terrible things, so it is easy to get those emotions and memories burned into your head, where they will live forever. I, like everyone else, had one of those awful, life-changing days I still remember today like it happened yesterday. I will never be able to forget every little detail and word from that day. It took some time after to realize what had exactly happened, how illegal most of it was, and the final magnitude of the lies and the effect it still has on my life today.

Sunday, December 27th, 1998, morning dawned crisp and bright.

I had passed out on the bed, lying at an awkward angle with my shooed feet dangling off the edge of the bed from my knees downward, when the annoyingly loud sound of someone banging on the front door filtered through my ears like in a dream. I groaned, opening my eyes briefly to be stunned by the brightness of the morning and promptly ducking my head under the pillow to avoid the burning glare and continue my sleep cozily.

I was almost drifting off again until, a few minutes later, the much gentler sound of tapping on my room door roused me from the semi-sleep-conscious state again. I cursed sleepily, turning to the door to cuss whoever the hell it was out, when my sleepy eyes recognized Diane at the door.

"What have you done?" A concerned frown knitted her brows, and her tone took on a pitch entirely different from the bland, nonchalant one I was used to. That cleared my head for a minute.

"Done? What...are you talking about?" I slurred, shutting my eyes briefly as the hangover from last night drummed through my head.

The previous night, like every Saturday night, I had closed Turn 4 Pizza, which meant I did not get home until after 1 am. As usual, I hung out with Mikey and everyone else for a few hours after work. I was not much of an alcohol drinker, but that Saturday night was different.

I had not talked to Shawna since her mom had ambushed me at Ricky's probation meeting, which left me feeling depressed, confused, worried, and anxious, among a hundred other emotions.

So that Saturday night, I had quite a few drinks, hoping to momentarily escape the stress and enjoy the company of my friends like normal.

"There's a detective waiting at the front door to talk to you," she announced solemnly and walked out, promptly leaving me to wade through the clogged, sleepy state of mind trying to figure out what a detective needed to hear from me on a Sunday morning.

I stumbled out of my room and onto the doorway leading out to the front yard, shielding my eyes from the glare of the morning sunlight as I went.

Sure enough, there was a man in a black suit, the detective it had to be, and another man. I froze in my tracks, the sleepiness evaporating from my head in instants, and stared frozenly at Shawna's dad, Chester, standing right behind the detective, a sickening smile plastered on his pudgy red face.

I glanced at the paper in Chester's hand and recognized it was the letter I had written to Shawna, asking her why she would lie. I looked behind the two men, a little down the street from where we all stood; I saw a car that belonged to Shawna's parents and a small burgundy unmarked car that must have belonged to the Detective right behind it.

DRINK IN ME

"You're Mr. Timothy, I presume," the black-suited man announced in a high-sounding voice as if he were reading the opening speech to an important event.

He was a short, thin person with bright orange-red hair that was thinning in the middle and curly on the sides, like you see on a clown wig. His eyebrows were almost white, kind of like an albino, and he had dark brown freckles across his nose and cheeks. He was a redhead and on the wrong side of the ginger attractive spectrum.

"I'm Detective Yellowbelly, and I'd like you to step out and let's have a brief chat...or, of course", he added, with a slight bow and wink, *"I can just bring you down to the jail and talk to you there."*

My beating heart was deafening to my ears. I faltered on the front steps, nearly toppling down to the last steps, as I prodded my numbed senses to follow the more assertive steps of the suited man.

"Where are you taking me to?" I asked timidly after I had finally made it down the steps while he continued out of the yard and onto the streets.

Silence. I peered closer at Shawna's parents' car and noticed the human form in the back seat, my dear Shawna, and in the front passenger seat, her butch-looking mother.

Suddenly, there must have been a little too much air in the world as my fear turned to panic and apprehension.

I felt cornered, like at one of those truth-or-dare parties when you can tell someone's planning to pull a nasty trick on you that everyone else knows about except you.

"Get in," he ordered, reaching for the door of the driver's seat and settling in.

I stood unmoving beside the car and watched him pull out a book from under the dashboard and a pen from his suit. "Coming?" his raised eyebrows seemed to question when I had not moved a spot since he got in the car.

He was not driving me to jail since he had produced a pen and paper instead, I reasoned, and hesitantly walked over to the passenger door and got in. No sooner than I shut the passenger door did he begin with his questions.

"Do you know Shawna?"

"Of course, I...."

"How long have you known her?"

"Three mon..."

"How did you both meet?"

"She called lo...."

"So, have you been dating?"

I paused. It had been only a couple of questions, but it might as well have been the general exams. His pen scribbled something furiously on the notebook he held.

That was quite a lot of writing for someone who had cut me off mid-speech for every question he asked me. Was it even legal for him to be interrogating me like this?

I sighed deeply, feeling the warm surge of annoyance rising from my belly, along with the marching band drum pounding both sides of my head.

DRINK IN ME

I turned away from the detective, looking through the windshield at Shawna's parents' car parked in front. In front of me, I watched Shawna's blonde tresses turn slowly to the side like she didn't want to startle her parents just yet. Then, a little more quickly, she propped herself up on the seat so that she was facing backward and looking straight at me.

There was a certain urgency in her eyes. I watched as she mouthed the word "NO" as her head slowly shook from side to side. No??! My mind reeled, puzzled by what she meant by shaking her head in that manner.

Just as abruptly as she had tried to warn me of something I didn't yet understand, I watched her lips mouth the words *"I love you,"* big and slow so I could make out what she was saying. For the first time since I had been rudely awakened from sleep, my lips formed a smile, even if it was the faintest and the most short-lived; her mean punk-ass daddy had just caught wind of her.

I stared, horrified at how far backward Chester cocked his big beefy arms, his hands balled into a fist, and just about to bring it down on his daughter. She must have noticed the shock on my face because her smile quickly turned to a confused frown and a wtf look right before the first blow struck home and hard.

"WHAM!!" right to the side of her unsuspecting face. My stomach churned. The blow had been loud enough for me to hear the damn thud from the hit and from where I sat in the detective's car. I could not see Shawna anymore; she had dropped down immediately in her seat, and I was left with a deep ache that tore at my insides.

The hit was so hard, and she dropped so fast that I was worried she was knocked out. I reached for the door handle and opened my door to get out and check on her.

But as soon as I had one leg out of the car, detective Yellowbelly snapped,

"What are you doing? We are not done here, and if you try to leave right now, I will drive your ass to jail. Now get back in the car."

"Did you see that?" I turned around frantically to look at the detective. I had expected a lot of not-so-nice things from him, but not the casual indifference in his down turned lips and the way he tilted an eyebrow upward, holding his jotter up at me as if to say, "So what?" He had seen it.

"What! Aren't you going to do anything about that?" I was trying so hard not to be impolite and raise my voice, but this was maddening, pushing my limits farther than anything ever had so that my words were drawn out and came out in a suppressed screech, strange to even me.

"This is what's important to you. This is what you need to focus on, Mr. Lytton," he replied calmly, shooting me a scathing, flat stare.

If I had doubted it before now, it dawned on me that it was not just 'something' that was wrong. It was every damn thing. I ignored him and looked back at the car in front, blinking away the pain that clouded my eyes. Big old Chester was raising his arm again and again, each blow giving off the same sickening thud.

I still could not see Shawna, but I knew it would not only hurt like hell but would feel so agonizingly embarrassing. A kind of frantic helplessness seemed to overwhelm me, my heart sinking beneath my knees and a ringing going off in my ears. I searched my mind for an answer to what was happening. Why would nobody try to stop this? I screamed inwardly, my eyes darting from Shawna's mom casually sitting in the passenger front seat to the suited detective staring steadily and unmoved at me. A violent hate surged up from my stomach and left a sour taste in my mouth.

If he could see something this heinous happen right before him and turn an unseeing eye, he was just as baseless as a person who would eat the shit right out of his own ass.

"Look you might as well save our time and answer the questions you are asked. Shawna has already confessed everything and now it's your turn. It's your chance to tell your side and what y'all did so it's in your best interest to cooperate." His voice sounded to me like trying to pierce through the more deafening sounds of blows and yells coming from Chester.

"You know what sex is right? So, tell me, how did it go?" he asked in a much louder, persistent voice that seemed to sting my skin. I sat there, the words lingering in the air, feeling the sting of each syllable as it echoed the physical violence unfolding outside. I took a moment, a deep breath that did little to calm my racing heart. The world outside seemed to narrow down to the space between me and the detective.

"Look, if Shawna lied to you about her age, it's no big deal; you won't be in trouble. I just need to know it wasn't rape, and you didn't make her. You know what I mean, right?" He spoke with a lighter tone as if we were now friends. I just kept ignoring him while looking through the windshield. I could feel his eyes still staring at me, waiting for me to respond and after a very long silent moment he continued,

"I told you; Shawna has already confessed everything, so you might as well tell me what kind of sex y'all did." he scoffed, tap-tapping his pen hard on the notebook. I could feel every word he uttered clash with the turmoil inside me. In that moment, it wasn't just the question that hung heavily in the air, it was the weight of everything unsaid, the consequences of truths twisted by perception. I wrestled internally with the knowledge of what was right, what was expected, and what was fundamentally human about my reactions.

His questions weren't just inquiries; they were accusations veiled in curiosity, each one a test of my integrity and understanding of the situation. I turned my head and stared into his eyes, trying to see if I could find any sign of a real man. But the smug look on his freakish face and the realization that he was not going to help Shawna or do anything about the situation made me almost lose it.

"If you already know Shawna lied to me about her age, then why the fuck are you asking me about it?! Shawna's parents knew my age this whole time and didn't say a word about anything until four days ago. That's the truth! So, I don't know what the problem is or why you are at my house on an early Sunday morning asking dumbass questions and ignoring a girl getting beat up right in front of you?!"

My voice was a mix of demand and plea and only a little lower than a full-blown scream.

"Look, boy," he snapped back, setting his notebook and pen down on the dashboard and turning to look me in the eye. *"Don't you get smart with me, or I'll throw your pathetic ass in jail,"* he whispered slowly and deliberately so I knew he was not bluffing.

"He's sitting there abusing a child, a female right in front of you, and all you can do is..."

"We have to finish here!" He cut in loudly, stressing each word. *"Or we can finish down at the jail."*

That was like the fourth time he threatened me with that. I stared out the windshield wide-eyed and numb. I was questioning reality as I watched Chester continue to yell degrading insults at Shawna while pointing his finger in my direction.

I shook my head in a daze of disbelief, and with a calm trance-like tone, I said,

"No. I think I need a lawyer or something." Yellowbelly chuckled under his breath and scribbled faster in his notebook.

"You don't need to speak to a lawyer son," he said in a gently patronizing tone, gentler than any tone he had addressed me in since I met him. *"Here, sign this,"* he finished writing, zapping crazily on the book with one swift motion of the pen and thrusting the notebook at me.

I took the book quickly, peering from the illegible scrawls on the paper to his blank face and back again to the paper.

"It's your statement. What you just told me."

"Alright," I muttered.

"Sign here, and you're free to go."

And that is just what I did. I scribbled my signature on the spot he had pointed out to me as fast as I possibly could and jumped out of the car before Detective Yellowbelly could try to stop me. Thoughts of Shawna and my desire to hit her father flooded my mind and propelled my legs toward their car. Chester heard me coming and, just as quick as I approached, dashed out of the car and came threateningly close to me.

"I wish you would hit me like that," I hissed as I stuck out my chest, balled my fist, and inched even closer to him.

"Please, hit me like that. Please do"

"What did you say?" he shouted, taking a step back with big round eyes and his mouth in an O shape as if no one had ever spoken to him that way.

"Fucking coward," I cursed, sensing his bluff. I glanced backward to see Detective Yellowbelly taking steady strides towards me, shoulders drawn up in exaggerated self-importance.

"You need to take a walk back inside the house," he announced, unsnapping something as he did. It could have been handcuffs, pepper spray, or his gun, whatever; I was past caring now. I shot Chester one more scathing glare that said, "I would rip your fucking head off and shove it up your sorry wife's fat ass," and stomped back to the car, making sure to brush past him as I went, and threw the car door open. I eyed Bertha disgustingly, swallowing to quench the bile rising in my throat, and turned my attention to the one I had come for.

Ever so lightly, I put my hand on her back as if it would help take the pain she felt away. I would have easily taken every one of those blows her sorry father hit her with. She was still lying on the seat, curled up tight in a fetal position, hiding her face and head as if waiting for more hits. I could feel her body shivering or crying. And when I touched her, she flinched, and she made a sound, a kind of weak moan of pain, followed by sniffling, and I just about lost it. My heart pounded hard enough to burst out of my chest as I turned from her, wearing a look that I am sure let Chester know I was ready to go.

He faltered a bit before stopping to square up to me. A small, mysterious smile played on his lips. He raised his hand and made a big circle motion while looking at the whole neighborhood and my house and said in a gentle patronizing voice,

"Look around, boy, you're pretty much a nigger, and you'll never be anything more. Nothing is ever going to change about that!"

I stopped, my eyes wide in shock, my mouth popping open in a slight O. Had he just called me that? At first, I wasn't sure I had heard him correctly.

I looked around, hoping a person within hearing range of us had just heard what he said.

"You're not good enough for my daughter," his voice, a guttural whisper, sliced through my thoughts like an iced blade. *"And I better never catch you coming to my house again!"* he added, shaking his head for emphasis.

"Well, fortunately for you, you're more than welcome to come back to my house again." I had gathered myself enough to find my voice again. *"About 6 pm tonight, and please, call me what you just called me now. I dare you."*

The neighborhood where I lived would have a large block party every Sunday evening, and there would be about 100 black people out there to hear what he called me. Chester's face looked around with a bit of worry at what I said. That's when Detective Yellowbelly grabbed my arm and told me to come on. I took one more look at Shawna, and she was still balled up in the fetal position, hiding her face with her arms. Seeing her like that, I have never wanted to punch or hurt another human being as badly as I wanted to hit Chester right then!! I wanted to hit him so hard that he would lay on the ground and ball up just like she was doing!

"You come on, get back inside your house and watch your mouth!" Detective Yellowbelly said firmly, snatching my arm up roughly and shoving me onto my house. I jerked my arm away from him, locking eyes with Chester one more time, the detective, before silently walking off to my house. I lifted the curtains in my living room as soon as I got inside. Chester and Yellowbelly were standing close to each other, leaning in and talking like buddies. My eyes burned as I watched them: Detective saying something and Chester laughing heartily. I have never met a man with a gun and a badge be as big of a pussy-boy as Yellowbelly. A couple of moments later, I watched Detective Yellowbelly and Chester shake hands, get into their cars, and leave.

GLASS #8:

"Better that ten guilty persons escape than that one innocent person suffers." - William Blackstone

I groaned, desperately trying to block out the incessant ringing of the telephone. It was still dark and freezing, and I had hoped to catch a few more minutes of sleep. The time on the clock confirmed my frustration. It was only 6 in the morning. I pulled the pillow tighter against my ears, seeking solace in its softness.

Just as I started to drift back into slumber, my bedroom door burst open, and my sister Jennifer appeared, annoyed and half-asleep. She mumbled groggily,

"Hey, Tim, there's someone on the phone for you."

"Huh?" I mumbled, unsure if I had heard her correctly.

"Yeah, a telephone call for you. I think it's your girlfriend. I didn't ask her name, and it's 6 in the morning. I'm going back to sleep," she replied, dragging her feet as she retreated to her room.

I glanced at the clock once more, confirming the early hour, 6:02. With a sense of dread creeping in, I made my way to the phone. Thoughts of Shawna flooded my mind. Why would she be calling me at this ungodly hour? Was something wrong? Was she in trouble? A knot formed in my stomach, signaling that something was not right.

DRINK IN ME

I picked up the phone, my voice barely above a whisper, and greeted,

"Hello?"

"Hey," came Shawna's voice, filled with deep sobs. *"My dad made me call you. I told him I didn't want to, but he forced me. The detective is coming to arrest you,"* she managed to utter amidst her tears.

"Are you serious?" I asked, my mind struggling to comprehend.

"Yes, they're on their way to your house right now," she confirmed.

"What for?"

"I don't know why or what for. My dad is just laughing and saying that you have no idea who you're messing with." Her voice broke, each word punctuated by a sniffle.

"What are you going to do?"

"What can I do, Shawna..." I trailed off, feeling helpless.

BANG!!, BANG!!, BANG!! Suddenly, the sound of pounding fists against my front door jolted me, causing me to jump in surprise. The force of the hits made the pictures on the wall beside the door bounce.

"I have to go, Shawna... Someone is beating on my front door," I said gently. Her crying became almost hysterical, and I could barely understand her saying, "I'm so sorry," as I slowly hung up the phone.

The banging on the door echoed in my ears, my heart racing wildly in my chest. I stood frozen for a moment, eyes darting frantically with disbelief washing over me.

I rushed to put on some jeans and a shirt, slipping into my shoes in a hurry. My hands fumbled with the buttons as I nearly collided with Jo on my way to the door. As I swung it open, there stood Detective Yellowbelly, accompanied by a uniformed officer.

"Turn around; you're under arrest for statutory rape," Detective Yellowbelly commanded, his tone devoid of sympathy.

The sheriff's deputy grabbed my arm as I spun around, swiftly handcuffing me with my hands behind my back. While they escorted me out of my own home, I turned to look back over my shoulder at my sisters, Jennifer and Jo, standing close to each other with fear and shock.

The deputy forcefully shoved me into the back of a sheriff's squad car while Detective Yellowbelly followed closely in his unmarked vehicle. As we drove away, I squeezed my eyes shut, desperately hoping this was all just a terrible nightmare I would soon wake up from. The Iredell County courthouse is right beside the jailhouse.

It is almost one building separated by a walkway in-between, the one Detective Yellowbelly is shoving me along on, towards the courthouse. I had never known my senses to feel so sharp, to pick the most intricate details of the surroundings around me, and it was even more frustrating because I just wished I would black out on what was happening instead.

The cobblestones on the walkway pricked my feet through my sneaks; a single ray of the sun escaped from behind dark, shifting clouds. My hands burned behind my back, my legs dragged underneath me, and one huge stone on the ground pricked painfully enough to cause me to stumble. Detective Yellowbelly cursed under his breath, pulling me up by the collar of my shirt hard enough for me to hear a rip in the garment and, with one final shove, thrust me into the cold, bright building of the courthouse.

My eyes squinted to adjust to the even brighter lights of this place, and partly because I could not bear to look at the passive judgmental faces of people.

Detective Yellowbelly took me to an expansive room inside the courthouse with a large wooden table, which you see in office buildings and used for board meetings. The table was lined on both sides with nice leather office chairs. All four walls were lined with bookshelves full of what looked like law books. I guess it was a meeting room for lawyers.

I sat in one of the big black leather chairs with my hands cuffed behind my back. I heard Detective Yellowbelly talking to some woman in the next room, and I heard her say,

"Alright, you got me out of bed and down here. So, what have you got for me?"

He answered her in a low, muffled voice I could barely make out, but I heard the word rape. She exclaimed,

"Oh wow, let me grab my camera."

I heard some shuffling and footsteps approaching the meeting room I was in. I was leaning forward with my head looking down in my best attempt to hide my face with my hands cuffed behind my back. I heard her walk up to the doorway and stop. She was right in front of me, only 3 or 4 feet away. She stood there for a minute, quiet and still.

I kept my head down, and my eyes squeezed tightly shut as if I was waiting for something to hit me. After a few moments, I slowly opened my eyes and ever so slowly lifted my head to see if she was still standing there. Just as I lifted my head enough to look at her face, at that exact moment and with the same motion, she brought her camera up to her face.

She froze for a second looking at me through her camera lens. I squinted my eyes in anticipation of being shot. But surprisingly, she did not pull the trigger. She slowly brought the camera back down, and for a few seconds, our eyes met.

I am not sure what look was on my face or what could have possibly been conveyed to her, but she had a look of confusion or bewilderment. Maybe the look on my face was so pathetic that she took pity on me. Whatever it was, I am glad she did not take my picture. I guess she was a reporter for the newspaper, and I could only imagine my ugly mug on the front page of our shitty newspaper. She slowly turned and walked away.

I heard Deputy Yellowbelly ask the lady if she got what she needed. She said yes, and I heard her ask how old I was. He answered that I was an adult, 18 years old. He came to the room I was sitting in and, with a firm jerk, grabbed my arm and pulled me up. He led me down some stairs and out a side door. He almost dragged me down the courthouse side steps and across to the jail entrance.

He stood there holding a tight grip on my arm as if he thought I would try and break away and make a run for it. He buzzed the little intercom, and the door unlocked with a loud click. I was ushered in as if he still had something to prove. He pulled me inside, and the metal door banged shut behind me. He took me in front of the judge and charged me with four counts of Statutory Rape. They booked me, took my fingerprints, mugshot, and all that.

It was my first time being in jail, and if you have never had the privilege of going to jail, let me tell you that you are missing out on a whole new world, my friend. It is a chance to see human beings act as close to raw human nature as possible.

DRINK IN ME

I love watching documentaries about nature at its most basic. Big cats like Lions, and Cheetahs are some of my favorites to watch. I find it interesting to watch how wild their life is and how they perceive the world around them and deal with just one fundamental aspect and life situation at a time. I like watching nature at its purest. I have always watched people with the same kind of curiosity.

Well, being in jail and the inmates already inside are a lot like those nature documentaries. It is as close to pure, raw human nature as you can get. For human beings to be inmates and be forced to deal with other similar individuals where everybody is stripped of all personal possessions and just thrown in a cage to survive all alone is probably as close to being on the Serengeti as possible.

It is a whole new and unique way of living compared to regular society. You must learn a whole new way of life and the ways of the people who are already there.

You must learn two sets of rules. You have the jail rules that the guards make sure you follow. And then there are the inmate rules. Whenever it comes to conflict, and you must pick which rules to follow, well that is simple, always choose the inmate rules. There are only a few MUST follow inmate rules. The number 1 and most important rule is don't snitch.

Number 2, mind your own damn business. Number 3 is do not gamble with what you don't have and don't borrow money you can't pay back.

In 1998, Iredell County Jail had two sections: the old part and the new part. The old side had those classic iron bars you would see in old Western movies, with small cell blocks that could hold only a handful of people— primarily women and medical inmates.

On the other side was the new part, featuring larger pods or cells capable of housing up to 30 men each. There were no luxuries like TVs, radios, outdoor time, exercise, or even decent food.

They had what they called the drunk tank or holding cell. It was a long, cold concrete room with two payphones, a steel toilet, and a hard concrete bench along the wall. When the guard put me in the drunk tank, it was just me and an older guy for a long time.

After a while, the door opened, and this young guy came in there whom I will never forget. His name was Ronnie P. He was a white guy, but I think he wanted to be a hip-hop rapper because he would rap to himself and speak with heavy slang.

He was short and skinny with a buzz haircut and some zig-zag lines cut in the sides and back of his head. He was loud, and his personality was huge and full of energy. Ronnie looked at me and asked,

"Is your name John something?"

I said, *"Na, why?"*

"You look like this guy I know, or maybe his brother. You look young as hell, man. Have you ever been in here before?"

I shook my head no.

"Yeah, I've been in every damn part of this jail, almost every cell."

He bolstered about it like it was some badge of honor. Ronnie was one of those people who loves to talk a lot. He told me how he got caught this time and why he was in jail.

He was riding with some powdered cocaine. He told me the cops chased him down, and he tried to outrun them on a moped, or as he called it, a "liquor cycle." Ronnie turned his attention to the older guy in the cell, calling him Pops.

Ronnie and Pops were dressed in the jail outfits, and I was still in my street clothes. Ronnie started asking Pops if he had heard what happened the other day in the jail. I could not help but wonder what the hell he was talking about. Ronnie kept on talking to Pops, saying,

"They fucked that guy up, man."

Pops was this older black guy sitting there, head slightly down, looking down at the floor, and did not say a word. He would nod his head like he was listening and seemed to be chewing on something because I remember wondering if gum was allowed in there.

Meanwhile, Ronnie was filling me in on how some poor guy had gotten brutally beaten recently. It was starting to scare the hell out of me, you know? I was already terrified of being in jail for the first time, and now I was hearing these horror stories.

Finally, after hearing Ronnie's' nightmare story, the door to the drunk tank opened, and they called my name. A guard escorted me across the hall to this tiny shower room, where I took a cold shower. He sprinkled that lice powder all over me. After that, I got dressed in that classic black and white striped jail outfit.

The guard handed me some plastic sandals for my feet and a small bag containing a travel-sized toothbrush, toothpaste, and deodorant. He grabbed some sheets, rolled them up in a blanket, and handed it to me. He walked me back across the hall to the drunk tank. About an hour later, they came for me again.

The guard opened the door to the drunk tank and called my name. Ronnie P. told the guard,

"Hey man, take me back to my cell."

"I'm not headed that way."

"Well, where y'all taken him?" Ronnie asked, his thumb gestured towards me.

"He's going to cell 187," the guard announced, almost cheerful.

Hearing the cell number made Pop's head rise up and Ronnie's jaw drop down, while both expressed wide-eyed shock as Ronnie informed the guard,

"Quit playing, yo! That's the gang cell. Y'all know y'all can't throw him in there."

The guard snapped back, *"Sit down and shut up, or I'll make sure you spend the night in the drunk tank!"*

That is how the guards would punish inmates by leaving them stuck in the drunk tank for endless hours.

I could not decide what was scarier, the fear on Pops' face or Ronnie's words. I felt frozen, holding my bedding and supplies with both arms, hoping the guard was wrong. When I had not moved an inch, the guard motioned for me, snapped, and yelled,

"Let's go Lytton."

Reluctantly, I walked to the door, looking at Pops and then at Ronnie, hoping one of them could somehow help me as I was led out into the hallway. Ronnie slowly shook his head from side to side and gave me one last look as if I was a dead man walking.

DRINK IN ME

The guard led me through a maze of doors, and we walked past cell pods, a half-circle arrangement of cells with a central guard booth.

Approaching cell 187, I felt my legs shaking and dizziness setting in. I wondered if I collapsed, would they put me in the cell or take me to a hospital? My heart raced 1000 beats per minute, and I even thought about pretending to have a heart attack. I was trying to think of any way to avoid going inside. I felt like a little skinny gazelle about to be surrounded by hungry lions. There was a loud click as the metal 187 door unlocked.

The cell/pod was loud with the echoing sound of guys talking, playing cards, and slamming dominoes on the table. But as soon as the cell door opened, everyone froze and stopped what they were doing to get a look at the new guy.

It got so quiet you could have heard a church mouse farting. It was like time stopped for a few seconds. I could feel all 30 pairs of eyes on me and what must have been a collective "WTF" in the minds of everyone in the cell. The guard told me my bunk was over in the far corner.

I said, "Great," that meant I would have to walk across the whole pod. I slowly started walking to my bunk with legs that seemed to weigh a ton and were wobbly. The cell pods are not really that big, but my bunk seemed to be miles away. I tried to keep my eyes looking straight ahead on the floor, so I did not lock eyes with anyone, and I held my bedroll tight against my chest.

When I finally reached my bunk in the corner, I just stopped and stared at the wall for a minute, trying to get some composure and wishing I could disappear. That is when I heard this intense voice say,

"Hey, white boy, what the fuck are you doing in my cell."

My whole body froze, and I thought I was going to pass out. I think my heart dropped to the floor, and I was stuck in that moment of fear when your eyes get as wide as they can open, and you are completely still, wondering what to do next. I slowly turned around, thinking, "This is it; this is where I'm going to die."

When I finished turning around, and I saw who the voice belonged to, I was so relieved to see someone whom I knew and someone who didn't want to kill me.

His name was Melvin. We weren't good friends, but we knew each other. He had a little brother named Cory, and they used to come over to my house and play football and basketball with us a lot.

And just a few months earlier, during the summer, on one hot day, I was on my way home driving Joann's car. Mel and his brother were walking, and they saw me and flagged me down for a ride. Their grandmother lived right down the road from my house, so I stopped and gave them a ride. Melvin laughed,

"Damn, I didn't think you could get any whiter than you already are, but your face is Casper white!"

"I thought I was going to die. You scared the hell out of me," I admitted, still feeling the leftover adrenaline shake through my body.

"They don't normally put regular dudes in this pod. For real. Did you piss off one of the guards or something?" he asked, crossing his arms.

"What the hell are you even doing in here?"

"I don't know anyone who works at the jail," I said, handing him my warrant.

113

Melvin glanced at it and shook his head. *"Damn, man. That's messed up. Is she related to the sheriff?"*

"I don't know. Why?" I asked, already feeling the weight of whatever connection Melvin was about to drop on me. He flipped the paper back toward me.

"Her last name is the same as the sheriff. You might want to ask her." he said before walking off.

I spent two and a half days in the gang cell, and no one bothered me. My sister, Joann, had a friend named Patrick, and he asked his mom and dad to use their home as collateral to get me out of jail. He told them the whole story about the dirty detective and what was happening to me, so his parents said yes and put their house up to get me out on bond. It was New Year's Eve 1998.

GLASS #9:

"The only real prison is fear, and the only real freedom is freedom from fear." - *Aung San Suu Kyi*

Shortly after the new year, I met my lawyer for the first time.

The first words out of his mouth were, *"You fucked the wrong one."*

Not, "Hey, my name is..." Those are encouraging words that you want to hear from your court-appointed attorney. He was as old as dirt and had long gray hair coming out of his ears and nose. He had these bushy gray eyebrows, and he spoke with a smart-ass attitude and had a shitty demeanor about him.

He was supposed to be one of the best attorneys in Statesville but did not act that way. Anyway, this was the moment I found out who she was related to, and a lot of things started to make sense. He said again,

"Yea, you fucked the wrong one!" As if I had not heard him the first time.

"Are you referring to her dad?" I asked.

"Yeah, and do you know who her dad's brother is?"

"I don't know. Her uncle?"

"Ha-ha, Yeah, and her uncle is Phil Redmond, the Sheriff of Iredell County."

DRINK IN ME

I said, *"Oh shit."*

"Oh, shit is right!"

He started looking at some papers in a folder and said, *"It seems the only evidence they have on you is your own statement admitting to having sex."*

"I didn't write any statement; the detective wrote it. I only signed it foolishly, so I don't know what he wrote down or where he got the number four from to charge me with four counts. I was in a rush so that I could stop her dad from beating the shit out of her in front of Detective Yellowbelly."

I tried explaining, *"I was half asleep and wasn't fully aware of what was happening. And seeing Shawna get hit like a grown man right before my eyes. I probably would have signed anything in that situation without realizing what it was."*

My lawyer kept flipping through papers in the folder and said,

"Well, it seems Shawna wrote two different statements. The first one said nothing happened between you and her, and then after they showed her your statement, she wrote a second statement saying that she lied about her age so that you would date her."

I said, *"That's the truth, so I don't understand why I was arrested or how Detective Yellowbelly can write whatever he wants to and call it my statement."*

I told my public pretender the whole story and what happened that day with Chester, Bertha, Shawna, and the detective. How they all came to my house and how I was made to sit in his car while he threatened me and asked me questions.

I guess it didn't matter, though, because my lawyer was no help whatsoever, and he sat there with a look of 'I don't care', or 'I'm not interested' on his face. He looked more annoyed or bothered than concerned.

But while I was at the visit with my public pretender, my sister Joann asked how much it would be to retain his services, knowing a paid lawyer would do a much better job than a free one. He looked right at us, and he said as matter-of-factly as anything else,

"For $30,000 cash, you won't do a day in prison. That $10,000 will go to the judge, $10,000 to the DA, and I will keep the other $10,000 for myself."

My sister and I turned to look at each other with the same confused and shocked looks on both of our faces and asked the same question, "Did he just say that?" I could not believe what I had just heard.

Yea, I knew shady shit goes on in courts, and money does all the talking, but I thought shit like this was in the big cities and not some small town in the middle of nowhere.

"So, it doesn't matter about guilt or innocence or right and wrong? I guess all that matters is the great dollar bill."

Mary-Jane was there with us, and she threatened to go to the TV news and newspaper to bring light to what was being done to me. My lawyer quickly reminded her of what County she and the rest of our family live in and that things could get bad for all of us.

When he said that, I felt like my family was going to be targets of unfair harassment, and I was to blame. My lawyer said I was screwed, and there was not much he could do. Chester is the one pressing charges, and Shawna has no say in the matter.

The North Carolina law he called "poorly written" is not set up to protect both "teenagers" in case of something like this. He told me there is no defense for not knowing someone's age or even being lied to or misled.

I said I could prove I did not write the statement, and Shawna could testify to not only lying to me but also to getting punched in the face and beaten on that day. My lawyer said,

"Well, imagine what her dad would do to her if she tried to testify and help you." He continued, *"Also, do you and your family plan on moving to a different county?"*

Hearing those words and the thought of bringing harm to Shawna and my family was something I could not do. My lawyer continued talking, but I had stopped listening. I already understood what his message was.

I looked over at both my sisters and thought that, as a man and as their brother, it was my job to protect them. My lawyer was pretty much asking me what was more important to me. The truth, justice, and what is right, or the pain and harm that would be inflicted on the ones I care for.

But what my lawyer did not tell me at the time was that he and the sheriff were good pals who liked to play with each other at the country club. I guess he did not think that information was important enough to disclose. I felt doomed leaving my lawyer's office.

So, we called some other attorneys, talked to a few, and told them what had happened. There were 2-3 attorneys who would not handle the case because of who the family was, and the other 2-3 we talked to wanted the same amount of cash or just a little more.

There was no way for me to come up with $30,000 cash. I felt helpless and absolutely screwed. But the fun times had not even started yet. My life was just about to get a whole lot more messed up. It was one of the saddest things to hear. It was like no one cared about justice or truth. It was all about money or who you knew.

T. LYTTON

I returned to work at Turn 4 Pizza but had to drop out of school without graduating. It was the first of many things that were taken from me unfairly. I wasn't supposed to talk to Shawna or be around her, but she started running away from home every other day, and when she did, she would usually call me if the cops didn't get her first.

At that point, I felt trapped between a rock and a hard place. On the one hand, I had developed true, genuine feelings and cared for Shawna, and on the other hand, if I broke her heart and stopped talking to her, she could make my life even worse. Who knew? So, I just tried to keep the peace.

There were a few times when she had run away, and there would be Sheriff deputies at my house or my job interrogating me and abusing me. I did not trust the law anymore after what Detective Yellowbelly did to me by lying about me and giving that false report.

One night, when I was at work, I was returning from a delivery and pulled to the back of Turn 4 pizza.

Four Sheriff's deputies and four squad cars were back there waiting for me. I stepped out of Bernie's black Toyota Camry, and they surrounded me against the driver's door, so I was trapped. I was 18 years old, 5'9', and 150 lbs., and they surrounded me like they were going to fight me. One of the deputies was aggressive and demanded to know my name as soon as I stepped out of the car.

When I said my name, he grabbed my arm, spun me around, and shoved me hard against the car. He pulled my hands together behind my back and put handcuffs on me so tight I could not even move my wrists at all.

He spun me back around to face all four of them. They all looked so much alike that they could pass for brothers. Each of them had the same buzzed haircut, and each was overweight. The aggressive one said,

"Where is Shawna? Tell us where she is, or we will lock your ass up."

I said, *"I don't know where she is. I'm not allowed to talk to her. Y'all should be trying to find out why she's always running away and covered in bruises."*

That is when the aggressive deputy slapped the side of my face so hard that it knocked my hat off and left me seeing the black and white dots. The whole left side of my face was burning with a sting and there was ringing in my ear. I was stunned and dazed, and before I had time to recover he pointed his finger and pressed it into my cheek, pushing my head back, and said,

"We're not playing with you."

He then grabbed my throat right under my chin and squeezed my neck with his thumb and fingers, causing me to gag. He jerked me up so that I was barely on my tiptoes and slammed the back of my head on the roof of the car. It hurt like hell, and I felt my neck and upper back pop.

He held me pinned to the roof of the car by just the grip of his hand around my throat and the tips of my toes, desperately trying to touch more ground.

The position he had me in was extremely painful and awkward, and I was straining to breathe.

But it is what he did next that no real man would ever do to another man, no matter how angry they are. He kneed me right in the fuckin' balls, and he did not do it softly.

He then put his face so close to mine that his nose was against my cheek. Through what sounded like clenched teeth, he said,

"Do you think this is a game? If you don't tell me where she is, I will lock your dumb ass up!"

I didn't know where Shawna was; even if I did, I wouldn't have told him. He was squeezing my throat so tight I wouldn't have been able to speak.

I could not take it anymore, and I felt a tear roll out of my eye and across my nose. It wasn't a tear from being scared or so much of the physical pain, but more like a tear of rage.

Have you ever been so angry, frustrated, and burning mad that it is like extreme pressure building and building inside of you until it feels like you can't take it anymore, and you feel like you're literally about to explode?

But you have no way to release that energy bomb, so to keep your whole body from exploding in rage, the big explosion is just a tear.

There is a certain type of helplessness someone feels when it is the cops who are violating you. The embarrassment of having to take whatever abuse feels your whole body with an emotion that has no equal.

That is when I checked out of my mind. The deputy was saying something, but I had zoned out.

I was already looking up at the stars from the position he had me in, so just like when I was a little kid and powerless, I would go floating off into space, looking down on Earth.

I don't know how long he held me there or how long I was checked out, but the next thing I remember was hearing Mikey yell, "Hey!" as if he could do anything about the situation.

Mikey had walked out of the back door to Turn 4 Pizza. Surprisingly, Mikey yelling "Hey" did help because the deputy who was squeezing my throat and holding me up let go, and I got some relief.

One of the other deputies told Mikey to go back inside or he would be arrested for obstruction.

Mikey walked back in for a moment and came to the back door with two more employees. The deputies started to talk in a low whisper amongst themselves. The aggressive deputy said,

"You're going to ride with me and tell me places where she might be."

Still handcuffed, he shoved me into the back of a squad car, and we were off down the road. He drove me to Shawna's house, where I was left in the back of the squad car while he went and talked to Chester and Bertha.

I was still in the back seat, handcuffed with my hands behind my back, when Chester's neighbor came out and walked up to the squad car. He was an older white man with gray hair.

The back window was slightly down, and he asked me what was happening. I told him they were looking for Shawna, but she had run away.

He told me the whole family was weird, they would never say hello, and all he could hear was cursing and yelling coming from there all the time. He wished me good luck and walked away.

After a long absence, the deputy returned, got in the car, and started driving down the road.

He drove to a trailer park and asked some of Shawna's friends, and they found her in an abandoned trailer. He drove me back to Turn 4 Pizza, dropped me off, and left like nothing had happened.

That was not the only time the deputies physically abused me. About two or three weeks later, Shawna had once again gone missing, and as usual, I was at work, returning from a delivery.

There were no cell phones, so there was no way for anyone to inform me in advance or warn me about the sheriff's deputies lying in wait. Only two deputies were present this time, accompanied by two squad cars.

When I rounded the corner of the building and caught sight of the two sheriff's cars, I hit the brakes and stopped. The two deputies stood talking to each other, waiting for me. They could see me, and I could see them. For a split second, the thought of turning my car around and making a desperate escape crossed my mind.

But deep down, I knew it would only worsen the situation and ultimately land me back in jail, but I was afraid to pull up to them because of the abuse I suffered the first time.

 The pizza place where I worked was part of a small shopping center next to a Food Lion and a few other interconnected shops.

Behind the building, where pizza drivers parked their cars, there was nothing but a few dumpsters and a dense patch of trees.

After a few tense seconds of locking eyes with the deputies, I realized it was Deputy "Low Blow," the same officer who had assaulted me before.

He circled his squad car and opened the driver's door, shooting me the dirtiest looks. I could sense his anticipation; perhaps he was hoping I would make a run for it.

I cautiously approached them, taking my time, silently hoping someone would come out the back door of Turn 4. When I reached the deputies, I parked the car and turned off the engine, and by the time I got my seat belt off, they were right on top of the driver's door.

The moment I began to slowly open the door, Deputy "Low Blow" violently jerked it open, leaned in, and grabbed my arm and the back of my shirt near my neck. With all his might, he yanked me out of the car, slinging me down on the hard asphalt.

The impact was brutal, embedding tiny rocks into my skin as I instinctively extended my hand to try and cushion the fall. My head and face still collided with the asphalt and left me stunned for a second while my knees and hand suffered severe scrapes that began to bleed from the force of being thrown down like a rag-doll.

"Low blow," with all his weight, drove his knee hard into my upper back, right between my shoulders, at the base of my neck, while his partner swiftly handcuffed me.

Pressing down the side of my face against the rough asphalt, he boasted,

"Oh, I guess you're not as stupid as everyone else says you are!"

He applied even more pressure, grinding my face against the gravel, using my head as leverage like a crutch to hoist his overweight, out-of-shape body upright and standing.

He grabbed me by my hair with one hand and my shirt collar with his other and yanked me up, causing my neck to crack unnaturally, and threw me into the back of his squad car. Once again, we were off, driving around, and I still would not say one word to the deputy: "Low blow."

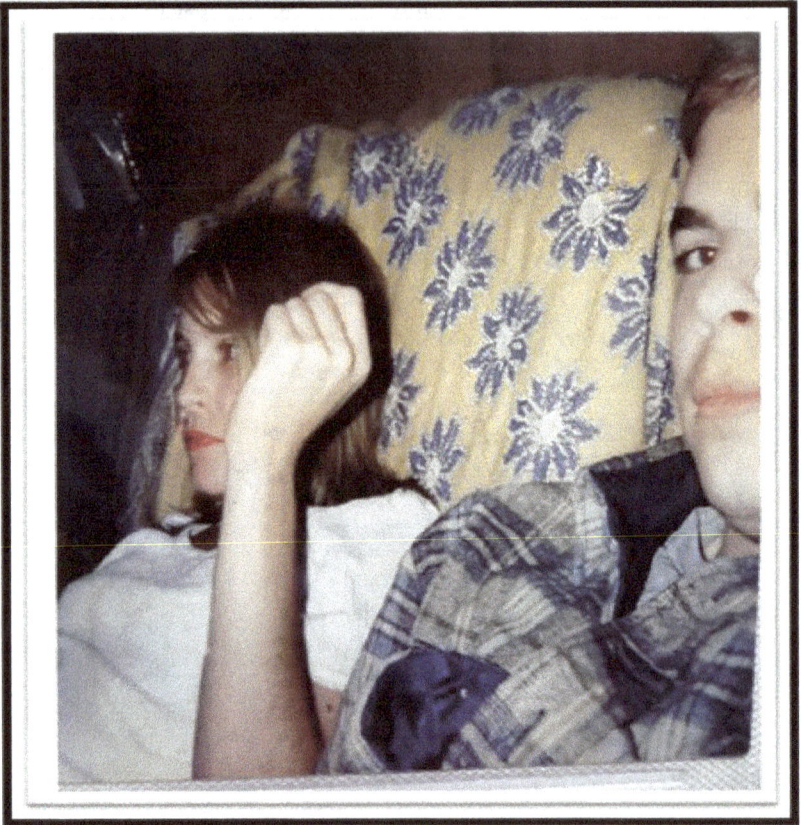

JOANN 24, TIMMY 19, 1999.

Out of jail on bond living at Patrick's

GLASS #10:

"When you're at the end of your rope, tie a knot and hold on." — Theodore Roosevelt

After three months of being out on bond, the continuous harassment and abuse I endured seemed to be escalating. My family and I were forced to find a new place to live after we were evicted from government housing due to the statutory rape charge.

Joann and I ended up moving in with a guy named Patrick, who was Joann's close friend. Patrick lived in the basement of his parents' house, which was like a separate little apartment with a bedroom, living room, bathroom, and space for two cots where Joann and I slept.

Patrick's parents had put their house up as collateral for my bond, the same house we were currently staying in. Patrick's dad was a retired police officer, and the day I got out of jail, I went to talk to him and thank him for putting their house up to post my bond.

Patrick's dad asked me about my situation, and I told him everything. What the detective did to me, Chester being the sheriff's family, and my relationship with Shawna. He apologized for what was happening and said he strongly disliked cops like Yellowbelly and the sheriff because it gives the good cops, like he was, a terrible name, and it takes away from the positive and trusting relationship society needs with its law enforcement.

Most nights, I would go to Mikey's house after work and crash there since Mikey and all his brothers worked at Turn 4 Pizza. One day, when I returned to Patrick's place, Joann shared an unbelievable and crazy story.

She said the day before, while she was watching TV, she heard a car honking outside and someone shouting my name. Curious, she went outside to see what was happening and found Chester holding a shotgun and standing beside Shawna, who was carrying a large duffle bag. Joann said Chester demanded I come outside and that he wanted to "talk" to me.

Joann told him he was crazy, and I was not there, and she was going to call the police. Chester hastily got into his truck and sped away, leaving Shawna behind with her bag. Joann approached her to ask what the hell was going on and noticed one side of Shawna's face was red and bruised.

According to Shawna, she had a heated argument with her dad about me, and he gave her an ultimatum to choose between him and me. When she picked me, he slapped her and ordered her to choose again. Even after she still chose me, he instructed her to pack a bag with her clothes while he loaded a shotgun. He forced her into his truck and drove her to Patrick's house, threatening to shoot me and then himself if she still chose me upon arrival.

A few minutes after Chester sped away, three sheriff's deputies and three squad cars arrived at the house with sirens blaring and lights flashing. Joann mentioned the deputies jumped from their squad cars, asking where I was and demanding to search the house.

Two deputies began searching the exterior and around the yard without permission. When I heard Joann's story, I felt fortunate I was not there, and I was glad I had spent the night at Mikey's house.

Nevertheless, I cannot help but wonder what might have occurred had I been there and stepped outside with Joann when Chester was angry and looking for me with a loaded shotgun. He should not have known where Joann and I were living then.

There is only one way he could have got that privileged information. Shawna was taken home by the deputies, and of course, Chester faced no legal consequences for physically assaulting his daughter or driving around with a loaded shotgun, threatening to kill me.

A few days later, I was sitting alone at Patrick's, and there was a knock on the basement back door.

I opened it, and there was Shawna. My eyes widened, and I looked outside to see if there was anyone else. She came inside, and I asked her what she was doing. Or how she knew where to find me.

She said she was running away and remembered where the house was from when her dad brought her over and dropped her off a few days ago. I told her she was going to end up getting me killed.

I felt bad for her; she could not get any help at home because no one would go to the sheriff's brother's house and question him. She asked if I could help her, and she wanted me to run away with her. I told her I was in enough trouble, and if I ran, Patrick's mom and dad would lose their home, and I could not do that to them.

I told her I could get her a hotel room for the night while she thought about it, but other than that, there was nothing I could do. About an hour after she was there, we heard the upstairs door open, so Shawna climbed under the bed and hid. Patrick's dad and a cop came downstairs and asked me if I had seen Shawna.

I said no, and the cop looked around briefly and he left. I felt terrible for lying to Patrick's dad after all they had done for me, but what was I supposed to do? Betray Shawna so she could go home and get beat like a grown man?

I called Patrick and told him I needed his help. I explained what was happening, and he came and took Shawna to a hotel. I went a bit later and spent the night with her so she wouldn't be alone.

Also, I hadn't had a chance to talk to Shawna about everything since her mom blindsided me at Ricky's probation meeting. Although I could guess the answer to my question, I still had to ask.

At the hotel, I sat in front of her on the bed so we could face each other and have an important talk.

"Why didn't you tell me your real age? Did you realize the trouble it could cause?" I asked, my voice laced with concern.

Shawna hesitated for a moment; her eyes glistened with unshed tears as she took a deep breath while her fingers nervously played with the tab on her soda can.

"I'm... so sorry. I just... I wanted to get to know you. I didn't think we'd click so well, that I'd like you this much."

She glanced up at me, then quickly looked away. *"I was going to tell you that day at the church, I swear. But... then we met, and kissed, and... Well, I got scared. I didn't want to lose you."*

Her voice cracked on the last word, and she fell silent. I sensed the sincerity in how she hung her head and her weak tone. My mind wrestled with itself because I wanted to be angry with her and had every right to be.

I searched inside to find that outrage, but for some reason it wasn't there. How do you get mad at someone for liking you so much they would lie to get close to you? I didn't know if flattery had me blind to the anger I should have felt or if there was no reason for it.

After a long moment, I asked, *"Why didn't you at least tell me about your uncle? About being related to the sheriff?"*

Shawna's head snapped up, her eyes meeting mine with a mixture of disbelief and sarcasm. *"Seriously, Tim? Would you have given me the time of day if I had?"*

I opened my mouth to protest, then closed it again. She had a point.

"When people find out," she continued, her gaze dropping back to her soda can, *"nobody wants to be my friend. Especially not boys. It's like they're all too scared."*

She started flicking the tab faster, her agitation evident. I reached out, gently tilting her chin up so she'd look at me.

"Is there anything else?" I asked softly. *"Any more secrets I should know about?"*

Shawna hesitated, her eyes darting away from mine. Finally, she took a deep shaky breath. *"There's... there's one more thing."*

My stomach clenched. *"What is it?"*

"I lied about my ex-boyfriend too," she whispered.

I frowned, confused. *"What do you mean?"*

Shawna bit her lip, tears finally spilling over. *"I... I've never actually had a boyfriend before. You're the first guy I've ever... you know."*

Genuinely curious I asked, "Why would you lie about that?" *"Because, I thought if I had told you the truth, you wouldn't have wanted me, so I lied,"* she explained. We both just stared into each other's eyes, the weight of the unspoken revelation hanging heavily in the air.

Shawna watched me anxiously, waiting for my reaction. She asked, *"Are you mad at me?"*

I didn't know what to say. I had asked for the truth, and now I'm not sure what to do with it? After a long and silent staring match, and still grappling with the information, I replied, "I'm not mad, Shawna."

We spent the rest of the night talking, figuring out our future, and how to accept not being together for at least a year and a half.

It was a painful conversation, but we both knew we had no other choice. We knew this would be the last time we could hang out together for who knows how long, and possibly ever. Neither of us wanted to sleep or think about saying goodbye, and we tried cherishing every minute we had together.

At some point during the night, I asked her why she kept running away so much. Shawna explained,

"I didn't know my dad would act this way, and I begged him to drop the charges and just let it go. I told him the truth and that it wasn't fair to you. I even told him I would never speak to you again, but he wouldn't budge. He enjoys making me cry over you every single day, and he wants to hurt you because it hurts me."

The following day, I asked her what she planned to do, and she said she did not want to go back home and that she couldn't take it anymore. So, I opened my wallet and gave her all my money, which was around $83. I hoped she would consider her options or maybe even go back home. We hugged and kissed before parting ways.

Shawna stood in the doorway with tears in her eyes, watching until I was out of sight.

My heart broke, and I felt utterly helpless. A few days later, I heard they had found her near the hotel.

She was taken to a hospital and forcibly admitted. I felt incredibly down and blamed myself for not being able to protect her. It made me question my worth as a man. I felt like a complete loser, weak and hopeless. That is when I attempted suicide.

I borrowed Patrick's truck, and I went to work as usual. Mikey's older brother, Bernie, also worked as a manager at Turn 4 Pizza, and sometimes he delivered pizzas. He also had a 9 mm handgun he would ride around with. I was going to use his gun so I could make it as quick and as painless as possible. I looked everywhere for that damn gun. In the office, at work, in his car and I even went to his house and looked through his room. I could not find it, so I had to leave without it.

My backup plan was to buy enough sleeping pills, go to sleep, and never wake up. I stopped at a department store on the way and bought ten boxes of 30 sleeping pills each. I figured those would be enough. The cashier who rang me up looked at all the boxes and looked at me funny. I drove far away to the beach and got a hotel room.

DRINK IN ME

I started drinking some Mad Dog 20/20 wine I had taken from Mikey's house while I was there looking for the gun before I left. I started eating a handful of sleeping pills and another. I wrote out a suicide note, and that is about the last thing I remember.

Four days later, I woke up in the hospital. After I had started drinking the wine and taking the sleeping pills, I had to go to the truck to get a pen to write out my suicide note, and the hotel manager noticed my distressed state and stumbling around and called the police.

At the time, I was only 19 and did not care if I lived or died. The hopelessness and helplessness I felt were overwhelming. I saw no way out for me. I didn't have the money to pay for justice. I couldn't return to school or move because I had nowhere to go. I was lost and heartbroken, and I did not see any future for myself.

When I finally regained consciousness after sleeping for four days, I was shocked to learn where I was and how long I had been out.

The hospital staff kept me under observation for three more days, during which I was confined to a bed, wearing nothing but a paper suicide-prevention gown.

Although they removed the catheter that had been inserted while I was unconscious, they still would not let me go to the bathroom by myself, and I had to use a bedpan.

Being on suicide watch and having to rely on a bedpan felt degrading and humiliating, compounding my already heavy burden of shame and depression.

T. LYTTON

The private hospital where I was staying had a lot of snooty nurses who treated me poorly, except for one lovely nurse who was kind and smelled amazing. She was an older woman compared to me at the time, but she had a youthful face, and with her dark hair and nicely blended pink highlights, she had a natural beauty about her.

It was her personality that made her even more appealing. I found myself drawn to her, and whenever she came to check my vitals, I felt cared for and comforted by her kind and gentle manner.

On the sixth day of my stay in the hospital, I was lying awake in bed at 2 or 3 a.m., unable to sleep anymore, feeling dirty and desperate for a shower. My hospital room was dark except for the light from the TV and doorway. I waited for Nurse Smell-good to come in to check my vitals, and when she did, I begged her to let me take a quick shower. I broke down and confided in her, telling her everything.

I explained everything that had led me to this point: the other nurses' mistreatment, the traumatic events in my life, and my overwhelming sense of hopelessness. At that moment, I must have seemed like a complete mess.

As tears welled up in my eyes, I turned my face away from her, trying to hide my emotions. Nurse Smell-good took a long, silent moment to assess the situation before saying,

"Let me see what I can do" and disappearing from the room. When she returned, she carried a plastic tub filled with warm, soapy water and a soft sponge. I thought, "Great, now I must wash myself in bed," which only made me more depressed.

However, she dipped the sponge in the water and started washing my face gently, wiping away my tears. She continued by washing each arm individually, then moving on to my chest and stomach washing me slowly and carefully.

Despite feeling humiliated and ashamed, I could not resist as she pulled the blanket down to clean my lower waist.

The paper suicide gown had been torn apart from days of sleeping and moving around, and I had ripped off what was left of it earlier that day and balled it up, throwing it on the floor in frustration at not getting to go to the bathroom alone.

This left me exposed and completely naked under the indestructible suicide blanket. I felt pathetic and like a low life being washed by someone else in bed.

As she continued to wash my lower stomach and ribs, I lay there with my eyes tightly shut, facing away from her. But as her movements brought her lower just above my pubic bone, my thoughts shifted from self-pity to an unexpected sense of arousal.

Here was this beautiful nurse, with her delicate touch and intoxicating perfume, so close to such an intimate part of my body. With careful precision, she slid the blanket off one leg while keeping the other covered. Wetting the sponge again, she moved on to wash my upper thigh before making her way to my knee then back up to the top of my inner thigh.

As she did so, her hand brushed against my penis, and I froze in shock, I tried desperately to control myself and push away any pleasurable sensations. But at 19 years old, it was nearly impossible to control my body's natural response.

Despite my best efforts to think of anything else, slowly but surely, about the time she was washing my upper thigh on my other leg, I started to get an erection, and no matter how hard I tried to fight it, no matter what I tried to think about, nothing did anything to stop it from becoming fully erect.

I lay there with my eyes squeezed shut, my face turned away in hopes of hiding my embarrassing situation from the nurse. I know she sees my erection, and she knows I am not asleep. But there is no way in hell I am opening my eyes and turning to face this woman right now. I was stuck, not knowing what to do.

I even held my breath in a lame attempt to disappear. I am lying there with a full erection and my body frozen in fear, shock, embarrassment, and a touch of shame. I thought maybe she would be disgusted, angry, or offended, so I braced myself for her reaction.

Instead, to my surprise, I felt the warm, wet sponge slowly and gently move over my penis and testicles as she continued to wash me thoroughly. My arousal heightened, and any hope of controlling myself vanished. The sensations were too intense to resist, and her perfume only added to the overwhelming pleasure.

I fought against my body's natural response and I tried my best to hold off until she was finished but Nurse Smell-good continued to wash me thoroughly and with great care.

Eventually, I couldn't help it, and I lost all control as my whole body tensed up with the overly sensitive, "Please don't move at all" sensation while I was having convulsions.

I can only imagine how ridiculous I must have looked with my dramatic grabbing of the blanket in a white-knuckle death grip while my face cringed up with intense pleasure, and I groaned. She didn't say a word and waited patiently until my body stopped shaking and my face relaxed. She wiped me one last time, politely covered me back up, and quietly left the room.

I was left there to wonder what the hell had just happened. I didn't know if I should say thank you or I'm sorry. I wasn't sure if it had been her intention or if I could not handle being washed so thoroughly.

It didn't seem like it was her intention, and she hadn't provided an apparent motive or direct purpose. I think it was just an unusual moment that surprised us both.

Who knows, it doesn't matter to me. Whatever it was, it honestly took my depression away. It helped to release or relax something in me, and I felt more at ease with reality. I did not think about suicide anymore or feel the want to end my suffering. I felt better, and it took my mind off all the bad and my doomed situation for a bit.

A week or two after I left the hospital, I received a court summons accusing me of violating my bond by writing a letter to Shawna. Chester had found an old letter I wrote to her during the early days of our relationship, forged a recent date, and used it to revoke my bond.

The judge, who was apparently friends with the Redmond family, not only revoked my bond but also set it at an impossibly high amount of $100,000.

About a month later, Chester and Bertha showed up to oppose my bond reduction, but I guess the judge on the bench was not friends with the Redmond family. The judge suggested a trial to settle the matter.

Chester had to take the stand and explain why he had driven Shawna to my house, threatened to kill me, and called the cops to set me up. He was so arrogant and cocky he tried to justify his actions as if it was normal behavior for a father. He ended up making a complete fool of himself.

My sister Joann also had to testify about Chester and what had happened that day. At the last minute, the prosecutor began whispering to Chester and Bertha. To my surprise, the prosecutor announced they would call Shawna to the stand.

I quickly turned to look at Joann, sitting behind me, and saw the worry on her face as she muttered, "Oh no." You see, in earlier court dates, they had deliberately avoided calling Shawna as a witness because they feared she would testify in my favor. But now, they had changed their stance and wanted her on the stand.

Seeing Joann's concern made me anxious, too, wondering if they had somehow influenced Shawna and turned her against me. It had been weeks since I last saw or spoke to Shawna, back when I left her at the hotel before my suicide attempt. I had no clue what she might be thinking or how she had been affected. Shawna walked out of a side door, and as soon as she entered the courtroom, my worries vanished.

Instantly, a smile lit up my face when I saw the dress she was wearing. It was a long black dress adorned with small sunflowers. I had once told her how beautiful she looked in that dress, and she knew it was my favorite.

Therefore, when I saw her wearing it, I knew everything would be alright. I turned back to Joann with a smile, but she gave me a puzzled look as her worry lingered. As Shawna took the stand, she glanced at me, and I could not help but smile in return.

Her cheeks turned a shade of red, and she struggled to suppress her smile. The prosecutor began questioning her, but after just a few inquiries, it became clear she was not testifying against me. When it was my lawyer's turn, he did not need to ask her any further questions, as her responses to the prosecutor's queries had already worked in my favor.

The best part was that once on the stand, Shawna just simply told the truth about the letter being an old one. When Shawna was excused from the stand, the prosecutor claimed I had brainwashed and manipulated her despite it being their decision to call her as a witness.

Shawna is incredibly intelligent, and as it turned out, she had informed the prosecutor beforehand that if they put her on the stand, she would lie and testify against me.

That was their motive for calling her, but Shawna had made them look foolish with her testimony. I looked over at Chester, whose face was turning red with anger. The frustration on their faces was priceless. It was the only court hearing that went in my favor. The judge reduced my bond to $50,000, which was still too high for me to pay, so I spent the next four months in jail. I told my lawyer about the dangerous situation I found myself in after being placed in a gang cell.

One of the seasoned inmates, whom they referred to as a "jailhouse lawyer," told me I should not even be in that jail or have any of my court proceedings in Iredell County. He told me to tell my lawyer to request a change of venue due to the potential conflict of interest arising from the sheriff's family members being involved in the case.

I shared this information with my lawyer; however, he informed me that he had tried to have a change of venue but had been denied.

Strangely enough, I never heard him raise the issue during any of the court proceedings I was involved in.

In August 1999, my lawyer offered me a plea deal for 60 months of active D.O.C. (Department of Correction) time. He claimed he could not convince the DA to drop the charges to a lesser crime than Statutory Rape.

I told my lawyer I would talk to my family about it. He told me he had already spoken with my family, and they thought it best to get this over with. He said I had two options. If I wanted to take it to trial, I could spend the next year and a half in jail waiting to go to trial and take my chances in Iredell County court, where Chester's family has so much influence.

And, if found guilty, I would get a maximum of 25 years in prison. My heart sank as soon as I heard the words coming out of his mouth. It was like a punch to the gut. I had never been in real trouble with the law before and didn't know how the legal system worked. I was just a nineteen-year-old kid, completely out of my depth and far outmatched. But I didn't have much time to think about my choice before the sheriff's deputies came knocking.

They arrested not only my brother Ricky but also my sisters Mary-Jane and Jennifer. It was like the entire world was crashing down on me. All three of them had been charged with questionable and petty disorderly conduct and drunk and disorderly, but I knew deep down it was just a way to put pressure on me.

My family did not deserve to be harassed and bullied because of me. I later found out the deputies laughed and joked about having "four Lytton's locked up at the same time." I felt trapped and helpless. I couldn't turn to the TV news or the newspaper to expose the injustices I was facing.

DRINK IN ME

My lawyer made it clear we lived in a particular county, and things could get bad for me and my family if I did. Plus, I lacked the financial means to seek assistance from anyone who could potentially help me in any way. Given the circumstances, my lawyer tried to reassure me that pleading guilty was the best choice. I trusted him, but the thought of spending five years in prison was almost too much to bear.

Still, I knew I did not have much choice. I had no clue I was walking into a trap that would ruin the rest of my life. On the day I went to court, literally right before I walked into the courtroom, my lawyer handed me the plea papers to sign and casually mentioned,

"Oh, they dropped one of the Statutory Rape charges to 2nd degree Kidnapping. It's not a big deal. It's a lesser charge. They want you on probation after you get out."

"I thought you said the DA wouldn't drop the charges to anything less. What is 2nd-degree kidnapping anyways?"

"It's whenever you give someone under 16 a ride without their parent's consent."

"That's bullshit! I didn't kidnap anybody!" I protested.

"This is what they want, and the plea is already written. The judge and D.A. are waiting, and we're due in the courtroom now. Look at it this way, at least it's not first-degree forcible rape that carries a life sentence like they tried very hard to stick you with."

I exclaimed, *"WHAT!?"*

He continued, *"Oh yeah, Chester and the detective held Shawna in the interrogation room for over 3 hours straight, with no water or bathroom, trying everything to get her to say you somehow made her or forced her. The only reason you're not looking at a life sentence is because she toughed it out and stood her ground."*

His words hit me like a slap to my face. I rushed to the steel toilet in the cell and vomited. There was no bench to sit on, so I lay down on the filthy jail cell floor, feeling lightheaded and dizzy as if I might pass out. My stomach churned, and I could not fathom the words he had just spoken. The realization that the people I had put my trust in had orchestrated a scheme to ruin my life was overwhelming.

The justice system, which was supposed to serve, was manipulated against me just like criminals manipulated it to evade punishment.

The detective and sheriff's deputies, who were supposed to protect and uphold the law, had taken advantage of their power to harass and intimidate me and my family.

The district attorney, who was supposed to be fair and seek justice, had conspired with them to ensure the rest of my life would be ruined and that I would be marked unjustly.

The lawyer I had turned to for guidance had sold me out, blinding me to their ulterior motives. I thought my lawyer was on my side and that he was looking out for me.

I was oblivious to the truth, blindly trusting a man who was stabbing me in the back. I could kick myself for falling into their trap. They were all aware of the unfair, long-lasting consequences I would face, the uphill battle to avoid being labeled a sex offender.

They had put extra time and work into orchestrating this whole scheme to inflict as much suffering as possible and to ensure my life would be forever tainted. I was so naive, gullible, and apparently deluded at nineteen years old, that I believed and trusted my lawyer and everything he told me.

DRINK IN ME

I was so stupid to believe he had my best interest in mind. He never suggested any other alternative outcome, never offered any other defense, and never told me I could turn a plea deal down. He knew I was a poor 19-year-old kid who hadn't even graduated from high school yet, let alone had a law degree to understand what was happening. He took full advantage of my trust and dependency on his help and guidance.

That is one of the biggest flaws of being a Pisces. You believe that humans are inherently good, and you try to see the positive in everyone, giving so much benefit of the doubt that sometimes you are blind to the evil and cruelty in some people.

As if my life had not been challenging enough for the first eighteen years, it was about to get even rougher. Instead of graduating from high school and heading off to college for four years or joining the army and possibly adding something positive and worth value to society, I found myself sentenced to five years in prison, followed by three years of probation with the first six months intense-probation, upon release, all while carrying the scarlet letter of a state sex offender and a level 3 predator on the federal sex offender list.

Everything happened so quickly, as if I was being rushed and swept through the court system. My entire case took less than nine months to go through our court system, from charge to sentence to prison. I never had a chance to fully grasp what was happening. The weight of despair and the thought of suicide lingered in my mind daily.

So, with no other choice really, I reluctantly took the plea deal as my lawyer advised and prepared myself for the long road ahead, and I was shipped off to an unfamiliar place, a prison that would become my new reality.

GLASS #11:

"Behind every man who has been accused of being someone he wasn't; is a woman who had done something she shouldn't have." - Blythe Baird

At the tender age of 19, I found myself betrayed by my court-appointed attorney, and I was shipped off to Polk Youth Institution for processing.

Polk, a huge maximum-security prison catering to guys aged 18-25, was quite a different reality compared to county jail. I mean, if you had to be locked up, I guess prison was slightly better than county jail, but it's like comparing red apples to green apples.

At least in prison, you could enjoy some outdoor time, watch TV, and listen to the radio. But Polk was an entirely different world of it's own, and I had no clue how to navigate this harsh environment. I felt like an alien in a foreign land. The language, customs, and way of life were entirely unfamiliar to me.

I had to learn the ropes quickly, understanding the ways of the prison, its inhabitants, and the overall lifestyle. I kept to myself and like always I just sat back and observed everything.

Initially, because my charges were sex related, I was constantly on guard, thinking I had to watch my back and that someone might try to harm me or make me a target for harassment.

However, most prisoners are not as ignorant as you might think. Throughout my time there, I was never bothered because of my charges. Now, do not get me wrong, the actual sex offenders and pedophiles did face harassment. Those who had committed real sex crimes like rape and molestation were rightfully targeted. When asked about my charges, I never lied and always shared my story honestly.

I spent two and a half months at Polk, and when I finished processing, I was transferred to Morrison Youth Prison.

During my early time at Morrison, I received a few heartfelt letters from Shawna. She expressed remorse for what her dad was doing, professed her love, and promised to wait for me.

I wrote her back, telling her she should go and live her life and try to be happy. There is no point in both of our lives being miserable, and when I get out, we can talk and go from there. However, around the four-month mark, the letters stopped, and I heard her father had enrolled her in some reform school for troubled kids.

Morrison, a medium-security prison for young men aged 18-24, was primarily occupied by troublemakers. You had a group of young guys who seemed to thrive on causing problems, all confined together with no shortage of opportunities to raise hell for their amusement.

Morrison had not yet phased out cash and cigarettes at the time, adding fuel to the fire. It had a reputation as one of the most dangerous and violent prisons in North Carolina.

Fights were a daily occurrence; if a day passed without witnessing one, it was a rarity. Morrison even had a small high school that required inmates without a G.E.D. to attend daily classes.

There would be bells and even class changes. The whole prison was like a wild circus, yet I was there. I had to sleep on a bunk beside guys like 8 Ball.

8 Ball was a young dude who had beaten and robbed his grandmother, turned the couch over on her, and tried to set the house on fire. Yep, he got 48 months.Or there was Jerry, who was driving drunk one-night, acting stupid, wrecked, and killed his best friend. He got 52 months. Or Cory, who would touch his little sister and get 36 months. And there was me, sitting behind bars for 60 months. For reasons I could not fully understand.

For about the first year, it all felt like a bad dream. I could not believe what had happened to me was real. I thought any day someone would come and tell me, "You're free to go home now; we were just messing with you." It felt like any minute, they would come and let me out, realizing what bullshit had happened. That is how unreal and out of place I felt.

The guards were far from safe and were assaulted regularly. Those guards who toughed it out and did not quit were pretty much beaten into submission. Inmates did almost anything they wanted. None of the female guards were safe. Every single one would get what inmates called "gunned down" every day. That is when an inmate would just openly jack off to whatever female guard was on duty. It was one of the most disgusting and degrading things I have ever seen.

I felt sorry for the women that didn't like it. And yes, some women guards did like it. They would intentionally provoke inmates by leaning over desks or railings, poking their asses out, and swinging them from side to side, knowing that there is an inmate right behind you jacking off. Some of the female guards seemed to get off on being openly masturbated to. There were a few of them who would even sit at their desks, eating penis-shaped foods in an odd way.

DRINK IN ME

One day, I had a doctor's appointment and got out of GED school early, and in my dorm, it was just me and one other inmate while everyone else was still at school.

The guard working inside the dorm was a woman with long blond hair. She was working alone in the dorm, which wasn't unusual. It was time for the prison's headcount, something they did multiple times a day. During the headcount, no one was allowed to move around. This usually took 30 to 45 minutes. So, me and the other inmate are just lying in our bunks, waiting for the count to finish.

The woman guard walks into the dorm's bed area and sits at one of the small tables near our bunks. She pulls out a banana and starts peeling it slowly with her teeth. She would roll the tip of the banana around her lips, occasionally kissing it, and she would roll her tongue around the tip of the banana.

After that, she would take the whole banana, and I do mean the whole thing, and stick it down her throat, only to pull it back out whole and start kissing it again.

It was the strangest way I have ever seen someone eat a banana. I'm not going to lie, no shame; I found it strangely fascinating, even perhaps a bit arousing, and I was unable to turn away.

The other inmate had already jumped behind his locker door, and he looked like a bobble-head on a car dashboard. Meanwhile, she's still doing her thing with the banana, all while keeping eye contact with me. She suddenly stops, slowly pulls the banana out of her mouth, smiles, and casually says to me,

"If you're planning to do something about your 'tent,' you might want to start taking it down before the headcount is over."

Now, I can be a bit slow sometimes, and I'd never heard the term "tent" used that way before. So, I gave her a puzzled "WTF" look.

She just smiled and nodded toward my crotch, and I glanced down to see I had a massive erection sticking straight up. Now I understood her "tent" reference. She told me,

"You may want to hurry up and start working on that. Don't worry about me; I'm not shy."

Then she went back to her unique banana-eating. At first, I was in shock and kind of just watched, and after a few moments of looking at each other, she finally gave up.

In the end, I couldn't do it. I can't just masturbate out in the open and on-demand like some porn star for a woman I don't know, especially with some other guy standing only a few feet away and watching.

After a little bit longer, she realized I was not going to masturbate for her; she just stopped and stared at me, but with very different eyes.

I'm pretty sure I disappointed her because she stood up, pursed her lips, slowly shook her head, and walked out of the dorm, throwing the banana in the trash on her way out. I felt bad as if I had hurt her feelings or let her down somehow. I even tried apologizing to her and explaining I am not that type of guy.

From that day on, whenever she worked in my dorm, she ignored me and wouldn't speak to me or even look at me for more than a few seconds. She wouldn't even call out my name for my mail. If I had a letter, she would send another inmate to tell me I had mail, and she would just leave it on the desk for me to pick up.

DRINK IN ME

It was wild, so I hurried up and got my G.E.D. as quickly as I could. I got a job as a mental health janitor, and one of the job's major perks was my single cell by myself. Part of my job description was that the medical janitor and I had to go around and clean up blood spills from fights.

I had to clean up blood from a bathroom one time when it looked like someone had been shot in the side of the head.

There was blood splatter covering every portion of one wall, and there was a big pool of it on the floor. It was horrible.

My 21st birthday was hands down the saddest birthday I have ever experienced. I found myself locked away in one of the worst prisons in North Carolina. Instead of celebrating with friends and family at home, I was surrounded by what can only be described as a group of wild animals.

So, on my birthday, I bought myself a honey-bun, spread some peanut butter on top, and stuck a couple of matches in it as makeshift candles. I wished myself a happy birthday and retreated to my cell. Sitting on the bed, I ate my depressing cake while tears welled up in my eyes. I could only manage to eat half of it before tossing the rest away.

I turned off the lights and lay in bed. I tried to imagine what I would be doing at home, celebrating with Mikey, Jo, Mary, Ricky, and everyone else. My 21st birthday was on a Friday, so I could only imagine the fun night we would all have together.

But thinking about how the night should be was far too painful. I found myself lying there, trying to find a valid reason why I deserved to be there. Why do I deserve to feel the pain of absolute loneliness?

I searched my life for something I had done wrong, something to justify my situation and give me a reason to lie there and to cry myself to sleep. But there was nothing. I had not done anything to deserve this.

When I was 14, a group of us, including Mikey, Terry, and our friend Jeff, vandalized a couple of basketball goals. We got in trouble for it. At 16, I made the dumb decision to shoplift some sunglasses from a department store, but I was caught and punished for it.

That is the extent of my criminal activities. I had no connection to most of the guys I was locked up with. I knew next to nothing about drugs, apart from weed, and half the stuff they talked about went right over my head.

I could not relate or understand half the shit they would talk about. They would sit around, playing card games like Spades and Hearts, taking turns sharing their wild "War" stories about epic nights filled with all sorts of drugs and wild orgies with different-colored hookers.

My personal favorite was the daring police chases that sometimes ended in miraculous escapes or getting caught and landing them in prison. I wasn't a pimp, or hustler or drug dealer, or user, or thieve, or con man. I didn't do drugs and I didn't party with hookers. Hell, I had never even been to a strip club.

I had no such stories of my own, so I would just listen intently. Whenever I was asked about anything I was always honest. I was told by more than one inmate I didn't belong there. I felt like an outsider and I was truly alone in what seemed like a foreign land. There were moments when I seriously considered just giving up. Maybe fashioning a noose out of my bed sheet or using razor blades on my wrist.

But who wants to die in prison? Plus, I am sure it would only please Chester and his corrupt family. I had no choice but to stay strong and hold onto the hope someday I would receive redemption or retribution for all of this. Good karma. I thought there must be something later in life to make up for this injustice. Or at least that's what I hope and told myself.

Unless you have ever been to jail or prison or have a loved one incarcerated, then it is hard for me to explain what it is like in such a way you grasp the true emotion of being forced to live in a small cell and treated like an animal in a hord. The pain of having everything in your life stripped away and feeling alone and scared. It can break even the hardest of guys down, if just for a moment.

After spending nearly two and a half years at Morrison Youth camp, I was transferred to Newton Prison, to serve the rest of my sentence. Newton was a small, low-security prison for adults, and it was classified as an "honor-grade" facility. It was ten times better than Morrison. Although it was still prison it was way more relaxed and peaceful. Shortly after I arrived at the honor grade camp, it seems Chester had made a call to the prison, and was upset and complaining about me being given privileges.

He talked to the superintendent and my case manager and told them I was a dangerous sex offender and a threat who needed constant supervision, and I did not deserve any privileges. My case manager was the one who informed me about Chester's call.

I could not wrap my head around Chester's extreme anger and his relentless efforts to make my life even more miserable. This happened two and a half years into my sentence. As if he had not ruined my life enough already, it was overkill.

My case manager said he did not like the way Chester was speaking to him, and after he pulled my case file and saw the truth, he said it pissed him off so that's why he was telling me about it.

A few months after I got to Newton prison, and well over halfway through my sentence, I heard Shawna had a boyfriend and had maybe moved on with her life. A part of me was happy for her, and that she was doing well. Of course, another part of me was hurt to hear she had found someone else or had forgotten about me.

Mainly because I didn't feel as alone in prison until that point. It was like all the unjust and unfair acts were more bearable if I had her loyalty or as long as she didn't turn on me or forget about me. What I mean is, if I had to suffer Chester's rage and the lies from Yellowbelly, then at least I would have Shawna's love and loyalty or something to show for it.

That this tragedy wouldn't all be for nothing and that I wouldn't have to shoulder every bit of agony and torture for no apparent reason. I didn't want her to put her life on hold or suffer the torment that I was suffering.I wanted her to be happy and live life, but I didn't want to feel alone and forgotten, or cast aside like my ruined life had no value. It was a tough spot for a heart to be in and I guess it was going to hurt no matter what. I still had two years left to do in prison, regardless of what happened or how I felt. At Newton prison, I did the best I could to blend in, so to speak.

I would spend most of my days writing letters, play volleyball and basketball. But my favorite thing to do was play guitar as much as possible. It was my best escape from prison and I stole so much time from being incarcerated because I would lose myself in creating my own music and it helped, tremendously.

Not only was it fun and enjoyable but it was highly therapeutic and relaxing. It was also a creative outlet for all my emotions, both good and bad. I don't know how it was for the people listening and I didn't say it was great music, but it was my music and writing my own music not only made the whole world disappear but also made me smile.

I would get a visit every week from my family and friends. I could only have three people at a time visit so they would all take turns coming to visit me each week, and their love and support was the most important part of keeping me strong. Diane, all my sisters, my brother, my nieces Kim, Tiff and Marsai, also Mikey, his younger brother Brian and some other friends were all there for me and I'm very grateful for them.

I had a prison job working for the D.O.T (Department of Transportation), and for two years, I worked on the same road crew with the same man as my boss. His name was Bill, and we got to be like good friends. Working with him was what helped to pass the time.

He always took out the same four inmates every day and we would either pick up trash on the side of the road or flagging, stand in the road and hold the 'Stop/Slow' sign for traffic. We had to wear a bright orange vest that said 'INMATE' in big, bold letters across the back. Most people thought we were just regular D.O.T. workers until we turned around and they read Inmate. At first, I was so embarrassed and ashamed to stand out there for everyone to see that I was an inmate. But I told myself that I have nothing to be ashamed of.

I have nothing to feel guilty about, and if I do start feeling like I have done something wrong, I would be broken, and the dirty fuckers who put me here would win. So, to maintain my sanity, I did my best to have as much fun as I possibly could in prison.

154

I know how that sounds, and believe me it was no easy task given the gloomy prison environment, but I was determined not to let Chester and his allies see me defeated and miserable. Some days, I succeeded in having happier moments, laughing and smiling instead of dwelling on the injustice that had brought me here.

Of course, not every day was a win; I am only human, and some days, the weight of injustice and bitterness got the best of me, and depression would win. But overall, most days, I managed to find a reason to smile.

During the summertime, when we would stand in the road flagging, it was not as bad as most other days. We would wave and try to flirt with the women who drove by. Even though I wasn't the smoothest guy and I was hardly successful, I enjoyed the pursuit. It took my mind as far away from prison as possible, and it allowed me to reclaim a bit of my spirit from the prison's grip.

Finding any source of joy, like those warm, sunny days working on the D.O.T road crew, away from the prison and just the simple act of trying to flirt with women who passed by, was a way of stealing precious moments from being locked up and provided a much-needed escape from the prison. I was single, with no romantic prospects or affection.

As an inmate, you feel so unattractive, invisible, and unwanted. It's a painful feeling for any human being. I guess it's the purpose and part of the punishment, but it was a punishment I didn't deserve.

I did get a few phone numbers and addresses standing there and flagging. I saw a couple sets of breasts, from women riding by flashing us inmates. Some were great to look at and made you say thank you.

DRINK IN ME

Some were not as nice, but I was still grateful for the thought. I am not complaining. I even saw two vaginas while flagging, one of which looked more like a grey squirrel's tail than an actual vagina. I had some people give me cigarettes, candy, cold drinks, and money, and I was even offered beers a few times. I had people who would talk to me and I had people who would roll their windows up and lock their car doors. There was one person who made those long workdays a little brighter—Vicky.

She drove a bright yellow Chevy Camaro and had a presence you couldn't ignore. In her late twenties, she was attractive with an elegant figure, and almost neon green-looking eyes that seemed to glow. Her long, dark, curly hair, was simply gorgeous, making her stand out even more.. One day, as I stood there flagging traffic, Vicky drove by.

The cars always moved slowly, giving me a clear view of every driver passing through. It was the middle of summer and we were working on a quite country road that was bordered on both sides by tall, thick cornfields. As Vicky passed by me she waved and flashed me a warm smile. I waved back, and she continued on her way. A few minutes later, she circled back, now leading my line of traffic. She pulled right up to where I was standing and rolled down her window.

I'll be the first to admit—I'm not the smoothest guy when it comes to talking to beautiful women. Now, Bill, on the other hand, had the gift of gab and seemed to be fearless when talking to women. It would never work because he looked and dressed just like Panama Jack, complete with the hat and sunglasses, but with a big beer belly.

But he was so funny to watch and he had a way with words of making women laugh, even if it was from sheer disbelief at the things he said. Some were not as nice, but I was still grateful for the thought.

I am not complaining. I even saw two vaginas while flagging, one of which looked more like a gray squirrel's tail than an actual vagina. I had some people give me cigarettes, candy, cold drinks, and money, and I was even offered beers a few times.

I had people who would talk to me and I had people who would roll their windows up and lock their car doors. There was one person who made those long workdays a little brighter—Vicky.

She drove a bright yellow Chevy Camaro and had a presence you couldn't ignore. In her late twenties, she was attractive with an elegant figure, and almost neon green-looking eyes that seemed to glow. Her long, dark, curly hair, was simply gorgeous, making her stand out even more.. One day, as I stood there flagging traffic, Vicky drove by.

The cars always moved slowly, giving me a clear view of every driver passing through. It was the middle of summer and we were working on a quite country road that was bordered on both sides by tall, thick cornfields. As Vicky passed by me she waved and flashed me a warm smile. I waved back, and she continued on her way. A few minutes later, she circled back, now leading my line of traffic. She pulled right up to where I was standing and rolled down her window.

I'll be the first to admit—I'm not the smoothest guy when it comes to talking to beautiful women. She started telling me that she had just gone through a nasty divorce, and that's when Bill came speeding down to see what was going on and to say his cheesy lines.

Bill was cool about letting you talk to people, but he was going to be nosy for sure. He would not purposely run people off to be a dick. But his cheesy lines and corny jokes would make people want to hurry along.

DRINK IN ME

For the next week and a half, Vicky would come by every day and stop, and we would talk for a good bit. She would bring me and the other guy's cold drinks and even donuts one day.

She was friendly and sweet, and I liked her personality and getting to know her. Seeing and talking to her each day was nice and almost made me feel normal or free again.

On that Friday, our last day working on that road, I was flagging when Vicky's Carmaro pulled up. This time, she pulled beside me on the shoulder of the road and cut her car off. We said hello to each other, and she said,

"Come here; I've got something for you."

My first thought was another cold Pepsi, and I was thinking how sweet. I walked up to the driver's side window and saw she was wearing a short sundress. What she did next was better than any soft drink ever made.

She took her hands and slowly slid her sundress, which was already about mid-thigh, to begin with, and pulled it up to reveal she had forgotten to put on underwear. I could only stand there and drink in the refreshing sight before me.

As I stood there, stunned, Bill came racing down the road, having spotted her yellow Camaro. Vicky quickly pulled her skirt back down before Bill could reach us. He stepped out of his truck and approached us, immediately launching into one of his cheesy lines. Vicky laughed it off and shifted her gaze toward me but continued talking to Bill. That is when she said,

"Hey Bill, do you mind if Tim helps me find my lost dog? It ran into the cornfield, and Tim said he would help me find it."

Initially, my dumbass was confused because I had not seen a dog with her. But then Vicky gave me a seductive wink, and my slow train got on the right track. It caught me by surprise, and I did not expect she would say what she did.

I could see the look on Bill's face, and I saw the confusion and deliberation in his eyes as he processed the information, too. It took Bill a long moment to decide as he looked at me, at Vicky, back at me, back to Vicky, and one last time to me again. I guess Vicky could sense Bill had deep deliberation, and she said,

"Come on, Bill, Tim hasn't searched for a lost dog for over four years, so I can guarantee it will be one of the quickest searches ever."

The way Vicky raised her eyebrows, and chuckled while looking at me left me feeling confused. In true woman fashion like so many other women I have met in my life, I could swear she was both complimenting me and genuinely mock laughing at me, both at the same time.

Who knows? I was still trying to process the fact she wanted my help in finding her dog. But Bill said no, and it pissed me off, of course. I refused to even speak to Bill for a week. He said he told me no because other D.O.T. employees were working with us, and they would have gotten me in trouble.

I only had seven months left out of a 60-month sentence, and he did not want me to get caught or in trouble so close to getting released. Sadly, I never saw or spoke to Vicky after that day.

TIM 24, 2004

Newton prison two months before my release.

GLASS #12:

"The future depends on what you do today." - Mahatma Gandhi

On the 16th of May 2004, I finally emerged from prison, having endured five grueling years behind bars.

Stepping outside those prison gates, I took a long, deep breath of fresh air and let the warmth of the sun wash over my face. It was a moment of pure joy, knowing I had made it and now I had a shot at a new and better life.

Filled with hope, I believed I could leave the pain and trauma of prison behind me. Little did I know, the deck had been stacked against me years ago, and I was walking right into another trap. Waiting for me was my probation officer, Ms. Marionette, leaning against her white state car with an air of arrogance.

Her appearance did not inspire much confidence. She was a short, overweight woman with unnaturally flat, shiny hair and a hardened man-like expression. Her inauthentic demeanor reminded me of the many guards and cops I had encountered before.

Without wasting a moment, she asserted her authority over me. Throughout the ride home, she bombarded me with threats, listing all the things I couldn't do, shouldn't do, and better not do, and the dire consequences if I did. Ms. Marionette warned.

DRINK IN ME

"Do not contact Shawna. If you try to contact her, she will call the police and have you arrested. She is your victim, and she wants nothing to do with you. Do you understand?"

Her words caught me off guard. Shawna considering herself my victim and not wanting contact with me was a surprise.

"There's nothing saying I can't talk to her," I protested. *"She's a 20-year-old woman capable of making her own choices."*

Ms. Marionette shot me a mean face, with her tone more forceful.

"As part of your probation and as your PO, I am telling you to stay away from Shawna and all Subway restaurants in Statesville, where she works. If you try to contact her, you will violate your probation. Do I make myself clear?"

Shaking her disapproving head, she said condescendingly,

"Shawna is the victim of your crime, and she has a protective court order against you. Just like any other victim, she is traumatized and fearful of you."

Though her words were hard to believe, I had not talked to Shawna in five years, and I had just been released from prison, so I could not afford to take any risks. One of the first things I had planned was to find Shawna and see how she was doing.

But now I wasn't sure she would even talk to me. Ms. Marionette kept talking the whole ride home. I think she loves to hear her voice, but I stopped listening to anything she said. I was now wondering what had happened to make Shawna feel so bitter about me.

"I will see you at my office tomorrow morning; do not be late."

Her words broke my daze as she pulled into the driveway.

162

I had no choice but to stay with Diane and her boyfriend until I found a job and a place of my own. Just before stepping out of the car, I asked,

"Does Shawna's mother still work at the probation office?"

"Yes, Bertha still works at the probation office. She is the secretary."

"Well, isn't that a conflict of interest? Being on probation at the same office that Bertha works for."

"I'm a woman of God, and you have nothing to worry about. Bertha and I are not friends. I've already checked, and there is no conflict."

She spoke in an overly authoritative tone. I looked into her eyes, and something about her gaze did not feel comforting. It lacked the reassurance and honesty I had hoped for.

However, when Ms. Marionette dropped me off, it was as though all the happiness and hope I had felt during the ride home were instantly drained away by some joy-sucking vampire. I was desperate to escape my thoughts about my probation officer, if only for a little while.

So, I decided to go to Turn 4 Pizza and pay Mikey and everyone a visit. But walking into the restaurant after so many years away, I felt like I was 18 years old again. The memories of working there, filled with fun times and late nights, were so vivid in my mind.

Everything looked the same, yet it felt brand new. I saw the city map on the wall that still had a note I had written for directions on it. Seeing the same phones, I used to take pizza orders and talk to Shawna almost every night while I closed the store, which brought back a rush of memories and emotions I did not anticipate. It was all so overwhelming.

DRINK IN ME

The flood of memories became too much, and I told Mikey I needed to step outside for some air. He asked me to walk next door with him to Food Lion to look at a girl he had a huge crush on. I agreed but stepping into the store after spending five years in prison felt like being transported back to my first day of kindergarten.

An overwhelming sense of anxiety gripped me, making it difficult to venture further into the store where Mikey's crush worked as a cashier. It was a panic attack like nothing I had ever experienced before. Without a word to Mikey, I turned and bolted out of the store, my heart racing and my breath shallow. Mikey soon followed, looking both concerned and puzzled. I couldn't help but ask him, *"What's wrong with me?"*

Later that day, my family and friends gathered for a cookout to celebrate my release.

Even at my sister Wendy's house, surrounded by people I knew, I still felt out of place and unable to eat anything. The sun was setting, casting a warm glow over the backyard where the cookout was, while the smell of grilled burgers filled the air. Like I do at most parties, I stood near the edge of the crowd, nursing a soda. That is when a young woman with long dark hair and a warm smile approached me. She held a plate of food in one hand and extended the other towards me, introducing herself.

"I'm Angela, a friend of Kim's. You must be Tim. I've heard so much about you that I feel like I know you already." My nervousness began to ease as I shook Angela's hand.

"Yeah, that's me. It's nice to meet you, Angela."

She was an attractive Italian with long dark hair. She was short and petite with big green eyes and tan skin.

"You know, I must confess. The reason I feel as though I know you already is that I used to read the letters you wrote to Kim. I like your personality, and you've got a nice way with words."

I laughed, relieved by her lighthearted approach. *"Well, thank you. I hope I didn't say anything too embarrassing, especially about myself."*

Angela playfully nudged me and chuckled, *"Oh, there's nothing I can't handle. But don't worry; I promise I won't tell all your secrets."*

We continued to chat, moving effortlessly from one topic to another. Angela's easy-going Pisces nature made me feel comfortable, something I hadn't felt in a long time.

As the evening wore on, we found ourselves laughing together, sharing stories, and enjoying the simplicity of the moment. I began to relax and not feel so nervous and out of place. On my first night out of prison, I tossed and turned, trying desperately to fall asleep.

Lying there in the dark, I was haunted by the fear that if I did close my eyes, I might open them only to find myself back behind bars. My mind raced uncontrollably, a tangled mess of thoughts and emotions swirling inside me. I felt strong yet vulnerable, hopeful yet riddled with doubt.

Everything about the future seemed wrapped in a giant question mark. I didn't know where to begin or how to start rebuilding my life.

Thoughts of Shawna haunted me—I couldn't help but wonder if she truly saw herself as a victim, as Ms. Marionette had suggested during our car ride home. These persistent questions kept me awake, and by dawn, I was a bundle of nerves yet stubbornly determined.

Walking into Ms. Marionette's office the next day felt like stepping back into a world I desperately wanted to leave behind. Her tone was cold and distant. She seemed more worried about whether I would try to contact Shawna than about assisting me with reintegration into society. There was no mention of helping me find a job, no discussion of training or education opportunities, and nothing about any programs that might ease my transition.

They had put me away at 18 before I could graduate, halting my education. Even though I earned my G.E.D. in prison, Chester's phone calls to the prison and family influence had blocked me from joining any programs that could have given me trade skills or work experience.

Then, Released at 24, my only skill was flipping pizza dough. And now, I was expected to rebuild my life from scratch—no money, no skills, no experience, no degree, and no support from the state or probation. I was barred from setting foot on school property, which ruled out furthering my education or attending classes. I couldn't even work at places like McDonald's where employees might be under the age of eighteen.

Plus, I was supposed to do all this while carrying the stigma of a criminal record and being a registered "sex offender." To top it off, Ms. Marionette fitted me with a GPS ankle monitor for the first four months of my intensive probation. She said that the department was testing new technology, and I had no choice but to participate.

I was already anxious about going anywhere that was public but now i had to carry around this big black brick looking box with a long antenna sticking straight up. It was the receiver for the huge ankle bracelet that was strapped to me. It looked more like a bomb that I had to carry with me no matter where I went. Leaving her office, I felt a sense of entrapment that prison had never managed to instill—a different kind of confinement.

Although I was free from bars and fences, my freedom wasn't truly free. Every move I made was tracked, every place I visited monitored. I had no privacy. It was suffocating, all of it, and none of it felt deserved or justified. The only bright spot in my life was the weekends when I could escape the world, play music with Brian—Mikey's younger brother—and spend time with friends and family. Music was my way of forgetting everything.

Just like in prison, it wasn't only a means of feeling free but a way to actually have fun and be happy. I also started talking to Angela every day, and before long, our friendship blossomed into romance.

Desperate for any sense of normalcy, I moved in with her. But as the days turned into weeks, the challenges mounted—finding a job, mending relationships, and navigating the heavy burdens imposed by Ms. Marionette and the justice system.

It took months, a visit to the doctor, and a prescription for Xanax before I could begin to truly adjust to life on the outside. After the GPS ankle bracelet was removed and they could no longer track me, my life slowly improved, and I started embracing small moments of happiness.

Thanks to a family member, I found a job and saved enough money for a car. All the while, Ms. Marionette's efforts to send me back to prison became more and more relentless.

Every step I took toward bettering myself seemed to make her angrier, fueling her campaign against me. It was as if she resented me for not crumbling under the weight of her unfair demands. She used degrading treatment and constant reminders of my "sex offender" label to try and sabotage my progress, keeping me trapped in shame. She did all she could to try and make me feel like a crimanal or actual sex offender but of course it fully work. I couldn't relate to it, no matter how hard they tried to force that label on me.

DRINK IN ME

Ms. Marionette did a great job of degrading me and making me stressed with her power over my life and fear of her ruining it even more. She treated me like I was filth, making every interaction leave me depressed and hopeless. I knew what she was trying to do, and I did my best to mentally prepare for my visits with her, but she held so much power over my life that no matter how much I braced myself, she always left me feeling dejected and afraid.

She made my life a living nightmare, subjecting Angela's home, where I lived, to continuous searches that were incredibly embarrassing.

She even attempted to invade the privacy of my journal, which I had carefully hidden beneath my mattress. She administered drug tests almost every other week, something I had never even heard of before. Even with the GPS ankle bracelet on me, she still came by every other night to make sure I did not break curfew.

I remained in a constant state of depression and humiliation, feeling like I was always being watched, feeling constantly surveilled. I couldn't understand why she treated me as if I were "The Night Stalker" or some kind of predator. The worst part was that she knew the truth about why I was even on probation.

Despite that, she persisted in her relentless bullying. She even went as far as to demanded to see Angela's driver's license and scrutinized her age, despite her being 21 years old, as if she could be underage or something!

Her unrelenting bullying and shaming extended to my friends, to the point where they did not want to hang out with me anymore, and who could blame them? I was lucky to secure a job through a family member, but even where I worked, she would show up unexpectedly, embarrassing me and making my colleagues uneasy. It felt like I could not escape her presence.

T. LYTTON

It felt like I could not escape her presence. I tried reporting her to her supervisor and even went as far as contacting the Chief of Probation in North Carolina, but nothing was ever done.

I was met with lies and roadblocks at every turn. I felt trapped. With Redmond still holding power as sheriff, it was clear Ms. Marionette was just another tool in their hands, bending the law in their favor. I couldn't afford to move, and all my friends and family were in Iredell County. I couldn't afford an attorney, and even if I could, they were too afraid to stand up against the Redmond family.

The stress from my P.O.'s mistreatment became so unbearable that Angela and I separated for a brief period.

The stress, pressure, relentless harassment, and mistreatment kept building until it finally reached a breaking point around my birthday. I felt like I was going to crack. I desperately needed a break from it all, and my 25th birthday seemed like the perfect excuse to forget my troubles, even if only for a moment.

I was only 18 years old when I was arrested—I had never even experienced a strip club, or any adult bar or club. I wanted to feel free and normal, like a regular man, and have a bit of fun. So, I went out of town with Mikey and a few other guys to a club and had a few drinks.

I even got a room within walking distance of the club so I wouldn't have to drive home drunk. However, the mix of my Xanax and alcohol turned out to be a dangerous combination. I stayed at the club until closing, and with an early hotel checkout, I woke up still intoxicated and disoriented. On my way home, I dozed off and crashed into a ditch. I blew a .09 and was arrested. Charged with a DUI, I knew immediately it would violate my probation.

DRINK IN ME

One of the most messed-up things was that I didn't even enjoy the strip club. The women were beautiful, and I had fun, but the idea of paying someone to dance for me turned me off. It made me feel unattractive and cheap. It just wasn't my thing. I had only wanted to experience it. I made a mistake, and I had to accept the consequences.

But strangely, a part of me felt almost relieved by the turn of events. I had grown so exhausted from constantly living in fear, enduring Ms. Marionette's relentless harassment and mistreatment. As I was preparing for my court appearance for the DUI, I found out Angela was pregnant.

She began having complications with the pregnancy, and overwhelmed, not thinking clearly, I made the impulsive decision to go on the run to be there for her. I couldn't bear the thought of missing the birth of my daughter. It was one of the happiest moments of my life, and I wouldn't have wanted to miss it for anything.

Despite my fears and lack of knowledge as a first-time father, I knew one thing for certain: I would never be anything like Wayne. I couldn't even imagine treating my child the way I had been treated. Holding my daughter for the first time and seeing how small and vulnerable she was, my heart filled with love and nervous excitement.

Looking at her was enough to make me feel alive as if I had found a purpose in this world. The way she latched onto my finger with her tiny fist, as though she knew I was her dad. I remember the soft pink color of her cheeks and how she smelled like fresh laundry detergent. It was all so surreal, yet it felt natural at the same time.

I turned myself in a few days after my daughter was born. The D.U.I violated my probation, which meant I would have to spend 17-to-31 months in prison for the "2nd-degree kidnapping".

However, the added D.U.I charge meant my sentence was extended by four months. So, instead of a minimum of 17 months, I would have to serve a minimum of 21 months.

Since I already knew the ropes and how to do time, I kept my head down and served my time as best I could. It felt as long and as hard as the 60 months. Finally, after 21 months, my release day arrived, and I thought I would walk out of prison a free man.

Or at least I should have. As I walked through the prison gates, a deep sense of despair washed over me.

North Carolina law dictated I had to serve what is called post-release probation. The 2nd-degree kidnapping charge carried a 17-to-31-month sentence. Typically, inmates must work their time down from 31 to 17 by staying out of trouble and working a job or going to school in prison.

However, North Carolina implemented something called post-release probation. They automatically give a 9-month credit reduction from your maximum 31 months at the start of your sentence, in exchange for up to five years of post-release probation upon release. And you cannot avoid post-release probation unless you get into trouble in prison and serve your maximum of 31 months.

A lot of the inmates would either not work a prison job or purposely break a prison rule, get into trouble, and do the extra nine months instead of getting out with probation. Looking back, I should have done just that. Because not only was I released on probation yet again, but I was assigned the same probation officer who had made my life a living hell before, Ms. Marionette.

I felt like I was living in a nightmare. As I walked out of the prison gates for the 2nd time, I wanted to cry when I saw the sickening smirk on her face.

DRINK IN ME

I could see the joy and satisfaction in her eyes as she could see the fear and disappointment in mine. She seemed to get pleasure from my depression at realizing I was doomed. She explained to me with delight I could spend up to five years on post-release probation.

Like before, she wasted no time resuming her harassment, picking up where she had left off. I thought I was living in the worst Twilight Zone ever. Shortly after my release, we learned that Angela was pregnant for the second time, and just like before, complications arose with the pregnancy, adding even more stress to our already difficult situation.

I endured Ms. Marionette's treatment until my son was three months old. Then came the day I was home with the kids while Angela was at the grocery store.

Ms. Marionette showed up at our door, bringing with her a palpable tension that filled the air. Her sharp features were twisted into a malicious grin as she stepped past me and invited herself into our home without permission or hesitation.

"Just checking in," she said casually, but her tone held a hint of sadistic glee. My stomach churned with unease as she made her way towards the living room, where our oldest child was playing on the floor.

"Are you here alone with the kids?" She asked with a sickening smile on her face, her eyes flickering between me and our children. Fear crept up my spine as I realized what she was implying. I swallowed hard.

"Yeah, Angela is at the store, and I'm here with my kids."

I tried to sound confident, but there was a heavy dose of annoyance in my voice. Ms. Marionette's smile widened into a cruel sneer. It reminded me of the Grinch who was about to seal Christmas.

"You're not supposed to be alone with anyone under the age of 18," she said, relishing in the power she held over me. *"And you're not allowed to babysit any minors while on probation."*

The room fell deafeningly silent as we stared at each other with intense animosity. Her steely gaze and stern expression made it clear that the threat was real. She knew what she was doing. She knew I wasn't a danger to my own kids. But that didn't matter to her. The rules were the rules, and as long as she could twist them in her favor, she was going to use them to break me. We locked eyes, pure hatred radiating between us.

Later that night, I told Angela about Ms. Marionette's visit and I could feel the weight of stress and worry pressing down on my chest like a boulder. The silence between us was thick, suffocating, as I struggled to find the words. Finally, I whispered,

"I can't do this anymore. She is not going to stop… not until she's broken me."

Angela's hand tightened on my arm, her eyes wide with a mixture of fear and desperation.

"What are you going to do?"

"I've got to go back. Finish my time. Nine more months, and then… I'll be free from probation and maybe they will finally leave us alone."

The answer tasted like ash, and the dread hung in the air like a noose. I saw it in Angela's watery eyes, and I hated myself for being the one tightening the rope. The next morning, I made the call.

"Y'all win," I said, forcing the words through gritted teeth. *"Send me back. Just… leave my family out of it."*

DRINK IN ME

I could hear the smile in Ms. Marionette's voice, that sick, twisted glee that made my skin crawl. She didn't ask if I was sure, and didn't pretend to be concerned. She wasted no time in sealing my fate.

"Come by the office today," she chirped, as if we were arranging a lunch date. My stomach churned.

Later that afternoon, I stood outside her office. Angela and the kids were with me for one last moment. I clung to them like a lifeline, hugged them so tight I thought I'd never let go. But I had to. With one final breath, I turned towards the door, telling myself not to look back. But then, I heard it—my daughter's cry, piercing through the air, slicing right into my soul.

I turned, against my better judgment, and there they were: Angela, my children, all of them sobbing, as if the world had come crashing down. And in that moment, it felt like it had. I felt like a bad father for leaving my kids and a bad partner for leaving Angela alone with all the responsibility.

I have never felt so broken, so utterly useless and defeated. And so, for the third time, I found myself back in prison to finish my sentence for the "2nd-degree kidnapping" charge from 1998. This time, I had a flat nine-month sentence, but I refused to let it crush me.

I discovered every merit day I earned would knock a day off my sentence, so I threw myself into kitchen work like a man possessed. I worked two shifts a day, barely sleeping or eating.

I was determined to reduce my sentences as much as possible. In the end, I managed to bring it down from nine months to six. All three of my prison stints were for the same charges and plea from 1998. I was not a repeat offender, yet I found myself incarcerated three times for a total of 88 months. Sadly, even that wasn't enough for them to leave me alone.

T. LYTTON

GLASS #13

"Strength does not come from winning. Your struggles develop your strengths. When you go through hardships and decide not to surrender, that is strength." - Arnold Schwarzenegger

In 2008, after enduring a decade of agony, I was released for the last time at the age of 28.

There was a glimmer of hope in my heart. A decade had passed since I tasted freedom, and I was no longer burdened by probation or haunted by my 1998 charges, except for the requirement to register as a sex offender. I was free from the clutches of Chester, Bertha, and their puppetry of torment.

It was a chance for a fresh start with my two children, an opportunity to finally experience a semblance of peace and happiness. But unfortunately, someone was not going to let me be. When things started to look up, and I was finally experiencing joy and fulfillment in my life, everything came crashing down with a sudden knock on my door.

Opening it, I was met with the stern faces of a sheriff's deputy "of course", and a DSS (department of social services) worker standing on my porch. The deputy introduced himself as Deputy Whatever and introduced the DSS worker as Ms. Whoever, and he requested I step outside to speak with them. Suspicion and unease knotted my stomach as I followed them out, closing the door behind me.

Memories of the last time I stepped outside to have a chat with the police at the age of 18 came flooding back, causing my heart to race. Without wasting any time, Deputy Whatever got straight to the point.

"We received an anonymous call this morning accusing you of being violent towards Angela. Specifically punching her in the face while she held the baby. Is there any truth to that?"

Struggling to keep calm and not laugh at the ridiculousness, I replied, *"Are you serious? Of course not! Someone must be trying to cause me trouble."*

Deputy Whatever gave me a skeptical look while the DSS worker, Ms. Whoever pretentiously asked, *"Who would want to make up such a serious accusation about you?"*

"I have a pretty good idea," I replied with frustration, locking eyes with Deputy Whatever. *"I've never hit Angela, but I'm pretty sure if I did, she would have called the cops herself."*

Deputy Whatever snapped back, *"Save it. I hear these lies from guys like you all the time. Just stay beside my car and don't move. We need to speak with Angela alone."*

I knew trying to convince him of the truth was pointless, so I complied and stood next to the squad car. Through the huge front window of our house, I could see Angela holding our son in her arms while Ms. Whoever began talking to her. Their conversation was muffled from where I stood, but later, Angela told me what was said. She told me Ms. Whoever was gentle but condescending,

"We're here to help you, Angela. You don't have to protect him."

Deputy Whatever was more direct and forceful, *"I made him stay outside so you don't have to fear telling us anything. We know he is a violent sex offender, and we are here to help you. I can keep you safe, but I need you to tell us what happened."*

Angela was confused and taken aback, as she shook her head and responded, *"No...Tim has never hurt me or our kids."*

Ms. Whoever chimed in, *"Think about your daughter, Angela. Do you understand the danger of living with a convicted sex offender?"*

That remark was enough to set off Angela's fury, her fierce instinct to protect her family overriding her fear. She stepped forward, eyes blazing with anger, and shouted,

"Stop!! I know Tim. He is not who y'all are painting him to be. The only danger here is from people like you! Spreading lies and twisting the truth. Both of y'all are wrong for coming here with this bullshit, and both of y'all can get the hell out of my house!!"

The deputy and DSS worker were stunned, and I could see the expression of shock on both their faces. Realizing they wouldn't make any progress, they reluctantly left. I stood outside watching them go with a mix of relief and concern, but as Deputy Whatever passed by me, he muttered,

"We'll be back....soon."

Sure enough, a few days later, they returned with a mission to label our home as unsafe, claiming it needed repairs and calling it a hazard, even though my kids were perfectly safe and happy. It was a ridiculous and flimsy reason to justify their actions on paper. Once they had that excuse, they twisted every other aspect to fit their narrative. In court, one of the first things DSS said was, "Oh my god, he's a sex offender with a kidnapping charge," painting me as an actual criminal or threat.

They even attempted to portray me as lazy because I didn't have a job at the time, overlooking the immense difficulty I faced in finding employment and facing rejection at every turn.

As a result, my precious children were snatched away from me, and my relationship with Angela was pushed to its breaking point.

The unfair treatment from DSS, coupled with the pain and anger from being unable to fight back in court, had us constantly fighting with each other. It felt like a deliberate strategy, a divide-and-conquer tactic pitting us against each other. It was an incredibly challenging time, filled with heartache and pain. The loss of our kids hit Angela extremely hard, and initially, she was cooperative.

However, she eventually turned to drugs, sinking deeper into depression under the weight of despair. Her battle with drug use, triggered by the traumatic loss of our kids, led to her having to do a 90-day prison sentence. It tore apart our once-happy home. Eventually, the burden became unbearable, and we had to make the tough decision to separate for good.

Our family was left shattered, broken into pieces. I ended up with nowhere to go, trapped in a life that felt unbearable. I had no job, no car, no money, and no hope at all. I found myself living on my grandmother Lytton's couch. She was a Pisces and was sick, battling cancer. My efforts to secure a job were repeatedly rejected because being a registered sex offender kept showing up in my background report.

I clearly remember a job interview I had at a temporary employment agency. Initially, things went well; I felt good about how I presented myself and had a sense of relief. The interviewer, a kind woman in her late 50s with neatly tied gray hair, gave off a grandmotherly vibe. I was thrilled when she told me I got the job and would start on Monday. This was a big relief, especially because I needed work. We chatted pleasantly for a while.

But there was a knock on the office door, and another woman came in with a paper in her hand. She gave me a quick, smug look, but I brushed it off, thinking she might be having a bad day.

Still riding high from the news of the job, I didn't see what was coming. After a short absence, the interviewer returned, and her face said it all.

Her warmth had turned into a mix of contentment, disgust, and maybe even anger. Before she even spoke, I had a feeling of what was coming. Her voice was no longer friendly and soft; it had turned cold and formal. Instead of calling me "Tim," she addressed me as "Mr. Lytton" as she delivered the news in a curt, unfriendly manner. She said there was an issue with my background check, something the company could not overlook.

She asked me to leave, and I looked into her eyes, hoping to find some understanding or a chance to explain the unjust background report. But all I encountered was the all too familiar judgmental stare from someone who had already tried and convicted me in their mind. With no other choice, I hung my head heavily, shaking it in defeat, and silently walked away without explaining.

This situation had played out more than once before. The first couple of times, I would desperately try to explain myself, hoping it would change their minds or at least make them listen. But I quickly learned it was pointless. Most people did not care enough to listen.

Left with no other options, I decided to take matters into my own hands and clear my name from the sex offenders list. I had no choice but to file a petition in court and represent myself because I could not afford to hire a lawyer.

I believed any judge who looked at my case could see the dates, the people involved, the truth, and what it was, and would easily put everything together and remove my name from the list. But the judge's ruling was unexpected.

After thinking it over for three days, the judge rejected my petition because they were unsure about what to do about a technicality that may have put me on a federal list as a level three offender and someone who must register for life.

It was then I uncovered a deceitful move during my plea bargain in 1999, which explained the judge's hesitation and uncertainty. Let me explain the complexity of the situation.

There exist both federal and state sex offender lists. The federal framework has three tiers or levels, with the most serious offenders, those convicted of the most horrendous crimes like actual kidnapping and rape, classified under level 3.

States have to follow federal guidelines to access government support and other benefits. Any conviction for a sex-related offense combined with a kidnapping charge automatically elevates to level 3 offender status.

Once categorized at this level, removal from the list becomes an almost impossible challenge. The crafty district attorney who orchestrated my plea bargain took advantage of this rule, exploiting their authority and influence to position me as a level three offender, even though it was dishonest, and dirty, and they had to go out of the way to bend the law to do so. This manipulation of our legal system created an almost insurmountable obstacle for me to clear my name.

They were cunning and smart enough to cover their actions within the legal framework, so technically, it wasn't illegal, but it does expose who they are ethically as a person and their lack of decent morals. The district attorney wielded their power to appease the sheriff's family and at my expeince. They went above and beyond their duty to construct a deeply dirty and malicious plea deal.

They conveniently slipped in the second-degree kidnapping charge at the last minute to ensure I would not only be on probation under Bertha and Ms. Marionette but also stuck on the sex offenders list, wrongly labeled as a level three offender. Their actions were unjust and immoral, and they knew it, yet they abused their authority anyway.

As I vented my frustration and boiling anger to my grandma, I realized the extent of their wrongdoing. It takes a special kind of evil, heartlessness, spitefulness, and hatred to go to such lengths. The whole situation leaves me shaking my head in disbelief. Frustration and desperation consumed me, and I found myself saying,

"I wish the worst things upon those who have wronged me." I expected my grandmother to agree, but she surprised me with her response. She said,

"Don't wish bad upon them; pray for them instead."

She explained holding onto anger and bitterness only gave those who wronged me more control over my life and happiness. By praying for them, I could let go of my anger and move forward. At first, I thought she was crazy. How could I pray for the people who had hurt me so deeply? But her words stayed with me, and I started reflecting on why I was consumed by hate and bitterness.

It dawned on me that I was giving those people power over me by holding onto all that negativity. I needed to let go of the hate and control my life. Sadly, my grandmother Lytton would pass away from cancer only a month and a half later. She left some wise advice in my head before she passed because, in my moment of mourning, I did as she said, and I prayed for them. It wasn't more than a week or two later I finally lucked up and found a job. It was a rough, hard-working job, but I held onto it and worked my ass off to try and save my kids.

DRINK IN ME

I fought hard for almost two years to bounce back from living on my sick grandma's couch without a penny to my name and jobless to where I was two months away from getting custody of my kids. I refused to give up and kept pushing for the sake of my family. I passed every drug test, got my own place, found a job, and attended every meeting, court date, parenting class, and counseling session they threw my way. I even went through a sex offender evaluation with a psychologist. I went to great lengths to fulfill every requirement the Department of Social Services (DSS) set forth.

Slowly but surely, I started making progress. I finally got unsupervised weekend visits with my kids, but only after I signed a paper agreeing not to let Angela, the mother of my kids, visit or be around them. If I didn't sign, I'd lose those weekend visits and won't see my kids.

Around the same time, my sister Joann and her three young children needed a place to stay temporarily, and like a normal, compassionate human being, I opened my home to them. Joann had nowhere else to go then, and staying with me for a little while should have been no problem. That's what family is for to help each other. However, the DSS supervisor twisted this act of kindness into a trap, creating a sick demand she knew I would not obey.

I was only 60 days away from taking custody of my kids when she heartlessly demanded I make my disabled sister and her three young kids, all under ten years old, with the youngest not old enough to walk yet, leave my home. She suggested they go to a risky homeless shelter in the freezing winter.

Staring directly into my eyes, the DSS supervisor laid down an ultimatum: either comply immediately and make my sister and her kids leave or face the consequences of DSS stripping me of visitation weekends and my parental rights. It was a heartless demand.

How could I possibly turn my back on my sister, who has always been there for me more than anyone else, and leave her and her children without a place to go and without any support? The supervisor seemed to take perverse pleasure in the cruel trap she had set, her sinister grin revealing the twisted satisfaction of having me cornered in an evil checkmate.

As a devoted parent, I would go to any lengths and do anything for my kids to ensure their well-being. I had complied with every request and demand from DSS, except for one: I was unwilling to turn my back on my sister and be a heartless human being.

Ironically, DSS claims to prioritize the best interests of children. Yet, the workers in my case were attempting to force me into putting three innocent young children out onto the streets in the heart of winter. The position I was put in was not just incredibly tough; it was blatantly unfair and unjust, a situation nobody should ever have to endure.

Keep in mind my kids were never abused, neglected, or in danger. My kids were always safe, happy, and healthy. As I realized I had only one remaining weekend visit with my children, I chose to honor their wishes and allowed them to spend time with their mother. The entire situation illuminated a disturbing truth: DSS did not seem genuinely invested in reuniting me with my children. Instead, they appeared to be focused on discovering something I would refuse to do, merely to use it against me.

Witnessing their true intentions disgusted me. It is profoundly sad when a system designed to protect and aid people becomes an adversarial force we must battle against. I believe that someday, the truth about what happened will emerge. All these events took place when Redmond was still in power as sheriff, lending undeniable weight to the suspicion that these occurrences were far from coincidental.

DRINK IN ME

===

I want to shed light on the court document you are about to read and the deliberate attempt by DSS to tarnish my sister's reputation to justify their own wrongdoings and their reasoning for such a heartless demand. The truth is Joann's "drug convictions" are outdated charges related to marijuana from her teenage years and the 90s.

And the so-called "child abuse" charge that they wrongly labeled on purpose is actually a "child endangerment" ticket from the 90s, long before Joann even had children of her own. Here is what happened: Joann was looking after our niece when she accidentally climbed out of her car seat while they were driving. A police officer who was behind Joann witnessed the incident and pulled her over. However, it is important to note that the cop only gave her a ticket for "child endangerment" after Joann declined his inappropriate offer to go out on a date.

Now that the truth is known let us dig into the court document and see what DSS conveniently left out. They did not have a warrant to enter or search. Instead of respecting my rights and waiting for my presence, the workers pushed aside a 4-year-old girl and entered my home without permission. Joann explicitly told them to leave since I was not there, and they had no right to enter.

However, the DSS workers disregarded her and went ahead to conduct an illegal search of my house. It is worth mentioning the bag they claim to have seen beside my bed could only have been seen if they had searched my entire house. It is worth mentioning the bag they claim to have seen beside my bed could only have been seen if they had searched my entire house. Shockingly, all these details were practically admitted by DSS in the court document, which they shamelessly used as evidence to strip away my rights.

===

N.C. Supreme Court: N.C.

G.S. 7B-302(b): DSS/CPS may not enter a private residence for investigation purposes without at least one of the following: (1) The reasonable belief that a juvenile is in imminent danger of death or serious physical injury. (2) The permission of the parent or person responsible for the juvenile's care. (3) The accompaniment of a law enforcement officer with legal authority to enter the residence. (4) A court order.

Federal Court: During the ratification debates for the U.S. Constitution, the People demanded amendments (the Bill of Rights) to shield their fundamental rights from the federal government. This included the protection of home privacy. For this reason, James Madison drafted the Fourth Amendment, which states: "The Right of the people to be secure in their persons, houses papers and effects, against unreasonable searches and seizures, shall not be violated, and no Warrants shall issue, but upon probable cause, supported by Oath or affirmation, and particularly describing the place to be searched and the persons or things to be seized." After the Civil War, fundamental rights (including home privacy) were extended to limit state and local governments and federal officials.

The Supreme Court has vigorously enforced the Fourth Amendment, even to the point of excluding at criminal trials any evidence illegally seized by police without a warrant. There is no social worker exception to the criticisms of the Fourth Amendment. Federal Courts have almost unanimously found that the Fourth Amendment applies to officials from DSS/CPS.

5. That the minor children continue in placement in the licensed foster home with David and Christine ████ where they have been since June of 2010.

6. That the current plan of care for the minor children is reunification with the Respondent Father, Timothy Lytton, or termination of parental rights and adoption.

7. That Respondent Father Lytton continues to reside in a rental home and uses the maternal grandmother's vehicle for transportation.

8. That Respondent Father Lytton continues to work full time at McCaro Industries third shift.

9. That Respondent Father Lytton began unsupervised visits with the minor children for four hours on Saturdays beginning December 24, 2011. On January 24, 2011, he was allowed to have unsupervised weekend visits with the minor children.

10. That Respondent Father Lytton let his sister, Joann Lytton, and her children move in with him. Joann Lytton has previous CPS history, a criminal record and has been convicted of misdemeanor child abuse and drug convictions. He failed to notify the social worker that Ms. Lytton had moved into his home.

11. That the Respondent Mother was released from prison on February 8, 2012.

12. That on February 12, 2012, the minor children returned to the foster parents' home from the weekend visit they had with Respondent Father Lytton talking about "mommy".

13. That the social worker made an unannounced visit to Respondent Father Lytton's home on February 13, 2012. Joann Lytton's child, Peyton, reported to the social worker that the Respondent Mother went out the back door. Respondent Father Lytton was not home at the time. The social worker observed a black purse like the Respondent Mother carried in the past sitting on the floor beside the Respondent Father's bed.

14. That the social worker and social work supervisor went back to the home and knocked on the door. The Respondent Father was home and the Respondent Mother proceeded out the back door only to find the social work supervisor, Diane ████ standing in the door and the Respondent Mother cried, "Oh Shit" and slammed the door on Ms. ████.

15. That the Respondent Father and the Respondent Mother denied the minor children being in the presence of the Respondent Mother. Upon questioning her, Respondent Mother admitted she had bathed the minor children, played with them and put them to bed during their unsupervised weekend visit with the Respondent Father, Timothy Lytton.

16. That the Department advised Respondent Father Lytton there would no longer be any unsupervised visits with the minor children.

Actual court document and statement of the Department of Social Services.

GLASS #14:

"Drug addiction isn't about using drugs. It's about escaping reality."

Power and authority are two very important elements of our justice system, and those in positions of power such as law enforcement officers, district attorneys, judges, social workers, probation officers and sheriffs often wield that power for their benefit.

This abuse of power can be damaging to the entire system, leading to miscarriages of justice and a lack of trust in the people responsible for upholding the law. It is a sad truth that those in power can often take advantage of their position for personal or political gain.

This could be in the form of making decisions based on favoritism, bribery, and corruption or simply taking advantage of their authority to get away with immoral behavior. Power exposes the true character of a person.

Society places its trust in those who are tasked with administering justice. These people are given a lot of power and are entrusted with a grave responsibility to uphold justice and protect the rights of citizens. When this trust is betrayed, the entire foundation of the justice system is shaken.

The abuse of power by individuals in positions of authority can be incredibly damaging, often surpassing the harm caused by the very crimes they are supposed to address.

This misuse of authority has far-reaching consequences that extend beyond the immediate victims, their families, friends, and communities but can also severely undermine the integrity of the justice system itself.

Innocent individuals may find themselves wrongly accused, convicted, or subjected to excessive punishment. A glaring example is the wrongful inclusion of individuals on lists like the sex offenders register, highlighting how abuse of power can create systemic injustice. Instead of enhancing public safety, these lists often perpetuate discrimination against individuals who should not be on them.

The abuse of Child Protective Services is a growing problem in the United States, and nowhere more so than in Iredell County, North Carolina. These services are supposed to be in place to protect vulnerable children from abuse and neglect. Yet, they are often misused and manipulated to target low-income families or parents whom the department workers don't like.

This has led to a system of unfairness and injustice that is being perpetuated by dishonest social workers and a culture of "kidnap for ransom" racketeering in our courts.

It is no secret that poverty is a major factor in who Child Protective Services harasses and picks on. It is low-income families who are often easily targeted by Child Protective Services. These families are more likely to be seen as "at risk" due to their lack of resources, and social workers are more likely to take children into care just because people happen to be poor and unable to fight back against baseless allegations.

Dishonest social workers driven by personal biases and corruption can use lies to take children away from their parents just because they don't like someone or because someone does not kiss their ass.

Sadly, often, it is the same kind of person who has failed in life and is a sad human being that no one likes, including themselves. These sick individuals, in their need for validation and power, lack the emotional and intellectual capacity or ability to understand and exhibit true and honest compassion, empathy, and humility toward other human beings, especially children. They are wolves dressed as sheep and are given the power of the shepherd.

These people are cancer to a family and are playing with a human being's most valued and important thing in life.

These corrupt and dishonest CPS workers need to be stopped, and there needs to be the harshest penalties in law for those who are guilty of lies and dishonesty crimes that tear innocent families apart.

Why aren't the most severe and longest prison sentences given to those who are trusted authorities and have privileged power and abuse that power to break the law and purposely hurt innocent people? Why isn't there a mandatory sentence for those criminals in authority who break the law? Why do we give drug dealers and users such harsh prison sentences, but when it comes to government officials who break the law, commit crimes, and hurt people, even sometimes ruin people's lives forever, these criminals get a slap on the wrist, or often nothing at all?

We have laws that protect against almost every kind of discrimination except against people with low incomes and less fortunate. Poor people get the worst and most hurtful and damaging discrimination there is, and there is nothing to protect against people who are wrongfully discriminated against due to poverty.

==

DRINK IN ME

My kids were my reason for waking up, my only hope, and the greatest thing that ever happened to me.

Throughout my life, I had never truly felt wanted or loved just for being myself. My kids gave me that sense of love, acceptance, and appreciation without any conditions.

I have so much love to give, and they provided me with a place to pour it out, an authentic reason to live. My children were the great equalizers, erasing all the terrible memories of my past and making my time in prison feel like a distant memory. They gave me motivation, drive, and a reason to care. Our daily routine was a source of joy. I would get up, dress the kids, make breakfast, and put on their favorite cartoons. We would spend the day together, playing, learning, eating lunch, napping, and cherishing our time.

They were too young for school, and I could not find work then. Taking care of my kids was a job in itself, but it gave me a sense of purpose. When you take everything, a man has and his reason for living, he has no reason to care, and nothing left to live for. After my children were taken away, especially for the reasons they were, I lost all hope and surrendered to the overwhelming weight of life's struggles.

I felt empty, devoid of life, and lacked any hope of survival. I said to hell with it all, fuck everything, and I stopped caring about anything. As my depression deepened, I lost the motivation to face each new day, finding no appeal in getting out of bed. The burden became too much, overwhelming, an onerous load on a man's heart and soul. To cope with this despair, I turned to alcohol and drugs in an attempt to numb the relentless heartache and pain. I carried the heavy burden of believing everything was my fault, the reason why the Department of Social Services intruded into our lives, and why we endured such unjust treatment.

I felt like I, not Angela, bore the brunt of Chester's cruelty, unintentionally bringing chaos into our relationship. The labels of "sex offender" and "felon" only added to our challenges, putting us at an immediate disadvantage. I discovered powerful pain medication not only numbed physical pain but also dulled my emotional suffering.

I started taking these medications as often as I could, desperately seeking relief. However, even with the pain suppressed, I lacked the motivation and desire to leave my bed. It was during this time I stumbled upon Adderall, a synthetic amphetamine. Despite not having ADD or ADHD, its effects were quite the opposite of what those conditions typically entail.

It provided the energy required to face each new day. I began relying on Adderall regularly to muster the strength to confront the world. I could have been considered a "functioning addict," as I managed to maintain some semblance of a daily routine. Regrettably, my relationships deteriorated as I withdrew from society, consumed by shame and a persistent sense of failure, even though my family and friends knew the truth. I didn't hang out with Mikey or anyone else as much. I withdrew into my world of drugs and depression.

After about four years of depending on Adderall and potent pain medications, I found myself sinking deeper into the abyss through daily meth and Suboxone use.

I lived a life governed by needles and spoons for another four years. There were moments when I would flirt with an overdose, teetering on the edge, not because I wanted to die but because I didn't care to live anymore. I longed for an escape from the ceaseless torment of existence. I drifted through life in a haze, devoid of faith in the justice system and utterly despondent, fully aware of the darker aspects of law and order.

I felt defeated by life, as if Chester and all his accomplices had triumphed and taken everything from me, leaving me powerless to do anything about it. All of them, in their bid to gain favor with the sheriff's family, had succeeded in breaking me down completely.

I realized I did not stand a chance from the beginning. I believed Chester and his county associates had defeated me as both a man and a human being, crushing my spirit and making me ready to surrender, waving the white flag, and embracing a life of perpetual intoxication.

I felt like drugs were the only way of surviving. I figured that pain and depression could not fly as high as my drugs could get me, and as long as I could stay just a little higher than my pain, I would be able to exist or survive. I am not trying to justify my actions, but I want to shed light on the dire circumstances that led me down that perilous path. The decision to use it was all mine, and as a grown man, I can accept the shame and embarrassment that comes with it.

Most therapists or counselors say people turn to drugs to fill a hole or void in their lives, and there was a massive void in mine, a deep hole to fill. I felt alone, unable to fight back. Constant rejection and judgment from society had made it impossible for me to become a productive member. Despite my efforts to attend college, seek employment, and seek assistance, my status as a "sex offender" and felon made me undesirable, and it seemed like no one would lend a helping hand.

They took away the one thing that motivated me to get up every morning. Drugs became my crutch, my way of coping and surviving. I do not deny my responsibility for my actions as an adult. I chose to self-medicate and use drugs, and no one made me. I was exhausted and weak. I hated being reduced to just another statistic: a failure, an addicted junkie.

For almost eight years, I lived like a numb zombie, going through life in a blur. I managed to keep my drug use hidden from most people, putting on a fake smile and never letting anyone get close enough to see my struggles. Therapy or professional help was out of my financial reach, so I turned to self-medication as a means of coping until I could muster the strength to stand on my own as a man again.

I tried contacting attorneys, judges, and even members of Congress in my quest for help. My deepest desire was to see my children again, and I even tried contacting the foster mother. However, all my efforts seemed to fall on deaf ears. One day, my ex caught me in the act of shooting up, and it was the stark wake-up call I needed to quit.

I felt an overwhelming sense of shame, realizing I could not sink any lower. Living a life dependent on drugs with needles and spoons had become overwhelmingly exhausting and demoralizing. I felt pathetic, weak, and utterly sick of it all.

I learned about the sheriff's actions and how they were catching up with him. Coupled with the connections I had always suspected between the District Attorney, Marionette, CPS, and the sheriff, I realized it was now or never. I had to take action.

I faced a choice: succumb to self-destruction and end it all or summon the courage to stand up and fight back. I knew that if I did not pick myself up and at least try to do something, I did not deserve to live.

So, I decided to stand up for myself, to fight with every ounce of strength I had left. Deep down, I always held onto the hope that one day, I would have the opportunity to redeem myself and share the truth.

Initially, I was plagued by doubt and fear, so I hesitated to write this book. I had concerns for my family's safety, and I questioned whether a book could genuinely repair the damage done to my life—the years spent in prison and the lost time with my children.

But something told me to think about the next person. What about all those who may be facing similar struggles? What about those who have been wronged like I was? I thought about the future of society, the world my children will grow up in, and even the strangers I may never meet. They deserve to live in a world where authority is not abused, and justice is served. If my suffering can bring about some positive change or benefit for others, maybe it won't feel so pointless.

Also, I wanted to take away the power Chester and his accomplices had held over me for so long. The power to manipulate how people perceive me and misjudge me. The longer the truth remained hidden, the more control they had.

They weaponized the justice system and society's trust, using them as tools in their twisted game. By revealing the truth, I take away their power and expose their lies, allowing them to be rightfully judged. The shame they wrongly placed on my shoulders now rests on theirs, revealing their manipulation and abuse of power to the public.

From now on, anyone who tries to use the label or my name on the list against me will expose their ignorance and shed light on the corruption and flaws within our justice system. So, using everything as fuel and determination to pick myself up, I embarked on a challenging journey to find stable employment, get clean, and begin writing this book.

Pouring my heart, soul, time, and resources into sharing my side of the story became my sole focus. I was determined to let as many people as possible know my side. And that brings us full circle and to this point in my story, and to the part of the book where you, the reader, enter the picture, and we have come to know each other through these words you are reading right now.

'Hello there... Nice to meet you'. I am sure by now you have formed your own opinions and thoughts about me and my story, and that is okay. We all have different perspectives. I may never know what you think or feel, but I am grateful you have taken the time to hear my side of the story and to read my words with an open mind. At least now you have the whole picture and can come to your own conclusions.

That is what truly matters: the honest judgments people make about me, whether positive or negative. Either way, I respect your thoughts and feelings, whatever they may be. Because, at the end of the day, that is all I can ask for.

TIM 30, 2010

Living on grandma's couch.

GLASS #15:

"If you want to test a man's character, give him power." Abe Lincoln.

Let us take a moment to examine the consequences of my arrest and nearly eight-year prison sentence.

It costs the state of North Carolina approximately $40,000 per year to house an inmate in the Department of Corrections. And this figure does not even include the months I spent in the county jail.

For simplicity's sake, let's do the math: 8 years x $40,000 = $320,000 -- that's the amount of taxpayer money that went into keeping me incarcerated all those years. This figure does not even cover the additional expenses related to the legal process, from court proceedings to other associated costs in charging, convicting, and sentencing an individual in our justice system.

It's safe to say Chester's jealousy and personal vendetta cost the state of North Carolina over $320,000. That is a substantial amount of money that taxpayers had to bear to satisfy the ego of an abusive control freak who believed he was above the law and everyone else.

That is well over a quarter of a million dollars. Moreover, not one positive thing came from my arrest. His attempt to hurt me and ruin my life, accomplished what? I would say he did more harm than good. He put a tremendous amount of psychological pain and emotional guilt on his teenage daughter to have to bear and carry around.

Shawna is a good person, so she feels guilty. And every day I was in prison was another day she had to live with that burden. He hurt his daughter just as much as he hurt me, whether he was smart enough to realize it or not.

I cannot fathom how someone could derive any satisfaction from causing so much pain to another human being. But in the end, for what purpose? (1) Did I learn my lesson? Nope! What lesson was I supposed to learn? I take that back; I did learn a lesson: never blindly trust the police because not all of them are good or honest cops.

I am not saying every cop is dirty or corrupt, I know better than that. I'm saying don't be foolish like I was and assume all are good either. Also, always read what you sign! (2) Was the community safer with me in prison? Fuck no. There was nothing to fear from me, nor has there ever been anything to begin with.

I never hurt anyone. (3) Did society benefit from my incarceration? No, if anything, they took a young man who could have been of real value to society and tried to destroy a beautiful soul.

Hopefully by now I have earned enough of your trust and respect that you don't just dismiss my claims of having so many different parts of a county's departments used against me in less than fair or honorable ways.

That so many county employees would be willing to aid in questionable activities. It's hard to believe I know. That's why I'm simply sharing my side of the story and shining a light on everything and letting all of their actions speak for themselves.

===

In case you have not looked him up already, let me tell you a little about my county's good ole former sheriff. Back in 1998, there were no smartphones or cameras everywhere like today, ready to capture any moment. So, it may not directly prove my story, and although I cannot say that he personally did anything to me because I never interacted with or met him.

But I can say what his deputies and everyone else associated with him and his family did to me. Almost everything I have said is on court record and cannot be denied. For everything else you will just have to take my word for it. But after reading this and doing any research yourself, it should not be too hard to find my story below their standard of operation. I got all this from Google, which is all public information.

Phil Redmond was the sheriff of Iredell County, North Carolina, from 1994 to 2014. for 20 years, he got away with his reign of misconduct. One of the earliest controversies involving Redmond came in 1998 when he was accused of using racial slurs during a confrontation with an African American deputy. The incident led to a federal lawsuit and a settlement that required Redmond to undergo sensitivity training.

In 2003, Redmond was sued by a former deputy who claimed that he was fired in retaliation for reporting racial discrimination and harassment within the department.

The lawsuit alleged that Redmond created a hostile work environment and that he failed to act when deputies were accused of misconduct, such as making inappropriate comments and engaging in sexual harassment. The lawsuit was eventually settled out of court.

In 2004, the department was sued for tasering a pregnant woman, and the case garnered national attention and resulted in a $75,000 settlement. In 2005, he was accused of embezzling funds from the county and using them to pay for personal expenses, including a vacation to Las Vegas.

In 2006, Redmond was accused of using excessive force when he handcuffed and arrested a 79-year-old woman after a traffic stop in the town of Troutman. The woman claimed that Redmond threw her to the ground and handcuffed her, even though she was not resisting arrest. The case was eventually dropped.

In 2009, Redmond's deputies were accused of failing to investigate a homicide in which a man was shot while walking his dog. It was later revealed that the suspect in the case was a friend of Redmond's. The family of the victim sued Redmond and the Iredell County Sheriff's Office for failing to investigate the case properly.

In 2011, the Sheriff's Office was accused of violating the civil rights of a disabled man in a wheelchair.

The man alleged that a deputy used excessive force against him while trying to restrain him after he had attempted to leave the area. The deputy was later reprimanded for the incident.

In 2012, a group of deputies were accused of mistreating a Hispanic man in their custody. The man alleged that he was subjected to verbal abuse, racial slurs, and physical exertion. The deputies were suspended for their actions, but the lawsuit was eventually settled out of court.

In 2013, the Iredell County Sheriff's Office was sued for failing to protect a woman from her abusive husband. The lawsuit alleged Redmond and his deputies failed to investigate allegations of domestic violence against the husband despite being notified of the situation.

In 2013, Iredell County Sheriff Phil Redmond and one of his deputies settled a sexual harassment lawsuit brought by two women, one of whom was a domestic violence victim who had sought the officer's help, court records show.

Redmond and former sheriff's domestic violence investigator Ben Jenkins settled the suit in mediation. The other plaintiff in the case said Jenkins began sexually harassing and stalking her after he overheard her talking about her violent and abusive ex-husband, according to the lawsuit.

The lawsuit claimed that Redmond and the Sheriff's Office knew about the harassment and failed to take appropriate action against Jenkins and never provided sexual harassment training for its officers until three years after one of the woman's 2009 complaints. As far back as 2006, the lawsuit said, Jenkins had remarked that "Finding dates working with victims of domestic violence is like shooting fish in a barrel."

In 2014, Redmond was named one of the Nation's top 10 worst bosses by the website "eBossWatch." He was voted number 6 in the entire nation.

Employees cited a hostile work environment, favoritism, and retaliation against whistle-blowers.

One notable incident involving Sheriff Redmond and his deputies occurred in 2014 when it was alleged Redmond and several of his deputies had taken bribes from a local businessman in exchange for protection against criminal charges. In the wake of the scandal, Redmond and his deputies faced accusations of using their positions of power to intimidate and harass people in their community.

Shortly after, in 2014, Redmond was forced to resign from his position as sheriff after facing a possible criminal investigation and after mounting accusations.

One of the accusations against Redmond was that he was trying to influence the election process in the county by intimidating his deputies to vote for his chosen candidates. He was also accused of mismanaging the department's finances and wasting taxpayers' money.

Moreover, Redmond's approach to law enforcement was seen as unsatisfactory, as he was accused of using jail inmate labor to do personal work around his properties and not properly dealing with drug-related crimes, domestic violence, and other serious offenses.

He also did not properly train his deputies and did not provide them with the necessary resources and support to do their jobs properly.

Additionally, Redmond's administration faced criticism for implementing controversial programs like Stop and Frisk, which disproportionately targeted minorities. Issues and concerns were raised about racial profiling and violations of civil liberties.

Redmond and his deputies were accused of using excessive force, along with cronyism and nepotism, where friends and family members of Redmond were given preferential treatment.

Ultimately, the legacy of Sheriff Phil L. Redmond is a perfect example of how flawed our justice system is and how it seems to favor people with money, power, or status.

His behavior and the resulting controversy serve as a stark reminder of the pressing need for transparency and accountability in government officials, which underlines the importance of robust monitoring and policies.

Body cameras are a good start. Along with cameras inside every government vehicle, it will help ensure everyone, regardless of color, gender, religion, or economic status, can receive fair, honest, and just treatment.

It will compel those with special power and authority to do the right thing, cutting down on lies and abuse at the hands of those with power over regular citizens. I can also envision a day soon when it is mandatory for all D.S.S.

workers to wear body cameras while on duty. Imagine a USA where all police officers, detectives, judges, D.A.s, social workers, police chiefs, sheriffs, and correctional officers had to be honest and fair and do the job we entrust and pay them to do.

Those people in power and that have authority over the rest of us should not be able to weaponize the justice system or manipulate the laws and our courts to punish or hurt anyone for any reason they want too just because they can. There has to be a way to protect those who are victims of authority abuse.

There is a YouTube channel called "Audit the Audit" that showcases interactions between civilians and cops.

DRINK IN ME

While some videos depict officers doing their duties correctly and fairly, many videos show cops who lie, break the law, and plant evidence, among other injustices that, in days past, would have gone unchecked. Watching some of the dirty cops in action sometimes reminds me of how unfair it was for me when I was 18.

T. LYTTON

LAST CALL:

"In the end, we will remember not the words of our enemies, but the silence of our friends." - Martin Luther King Jr.

Today, I strive to live a quiet, low-key life. I wake up each day feeling grateful to be alive. Despite the challenges of still having my name on that list, I do my best to smile and appreciate each day. I remind myself that today is the only day that truly matters.

I eagerly await the day I can reunite with my kids and rebuild the natural bond a father should have with his children. If there is one thing I am sure of in this life, it is that my kids love me very much and I have saved all the court documents so that they can read the truth for themselves.

It took me a long time to speak up because I was genuinely scared for myself and my family's safety. I have no idea what kind of power they still hold now. The fear of something terrible happening to me, like going missing, facing questionable death, or being framed with false charges, almost kept me silent and from writing this book. A part of me is still afraid.

But I have reached a point where I can't keep quiet any longer. I have to stand up for myself. Staying silent only lets them continue their crimes, and it's time to expose the real criminals. I am tired of carrying around unnecessary shame.

DRINK IN ME

I will never get back the years I lost in prison, or the years unfairly branded as society's lowest scum. I am not seeking pity or sympathy. I do not believe the world owes me anything. I take pride in working hard for the accomplishments in my life. Life has thrown some sucker punches my way, but I am not just lying down and feeling sorry for myself and crying about it. All the bad and messed up stuff that has happened to me belongs to the past.

I cannot change what has already happened. All I can do is focus on being strong today. I am not weak, but unfortunately, nice guys are perceived that way.

It takes a severe toll on a man's soul to have too much empathy for a harsh and unforgiving world. So, this book is about sharing my story, putting the past to rest, forgiving, and letting go of the bitterness that has controlled my life for so long. I want to be a good person and do what is right for each day I have.

To be the best man and father I can be. I am going to continue to be Timmy, and I might not be cool or smooth or God's gift to women, but I am not a sex offender anyone has to fear. I hope this book brings some inner relief for me and some outer conviction for what should be right. I know there is no way to clear my name fully, but I hope this book will bring me as close as possible.

I might not have as much faith left in our justice system as I once had, but I have a lot of faith and trust in everyday people. I believe humans are inherently good; that's why helping others feels wonderful, smiles are contagious, and almost all babies are naturally happy. I think most humans are kind, decent, and have good hearts. When they read my story, they will see the real me, beyond the labels and assumptions, and judge me based on who I am.

In case you are wondering, I finally reached out to Shawna. I was hesitant to contact her due to the warnings from my probation officer, Ms. Marionette.

But out of care and respect for Shawna, I sent her a message explaining I was writing a book. I assured her I would respect her privacy and focus solely on the truth. I wanted her to understand my intentions were not to hurt her in any way and that I had no hard feelings toward her.

To my surprise, she was overjoyed to hear from me, and we talked for hours.

There was so much to catch up on, and we finally got to fill in the missing pieces of what had happened to each other. Shawna revealed she stopped writing to me in prison because her dad had threatened her. He said if she did not stop talking to me, he would find a way to have me charged with conspiracy to commit murder, and I would never get out.

He said he had the power to get me arrested and sent to prison for five years so he could find a way to get me charged with more. She said she was too afraid to contact me after my release because her mom, dad, Ms. Marionette, had all fed her lies.

They told her I was going around the prison telling everyone, even the correctional officers, that I blamed her for my imprisonment, and it was all her fault I hated her, and I intended to kill her if we ever crossed paths again.

Shawna said Ms. Marionette would come to her house, eat dinner, and talk to Chester and Bertha, telling them everything about me and keeping them informed of my day-to-day life.

Shawna said she truly believed Ms. Marionette because she was my probation officer and had direct interaction with me. In return, I shared with Shawna I was terrified to reach out to her because Ms.

Marionette had spun those same webs of lies, painting Shawna as my victim and convincing me that she despised me, even threatening to have me arrested if I tried to contact her.

Deep down, I suspected Ms. Marionette was lying, but she manipulated me by using Jesus to conceal her deceit. There was never a protective court order, and Shawna never felt like a victim.

Shawna could not hold back her tears as she confessed, we had both been robbed of all those years. I knew what she meant. It was one of the saddest things to hear. She told me she had taken one of my shirts without my knowledge when we were dating.

She said the day I was sentenced to prison, she was in her room crying and holding my shirt when her dad took the shirt away and started laughing in her face, bragging about how hard the rest of my life was going to be and that she and I would never be together. Shawna shared that she and her brother left home as soon as possible.

Sadly, her brother took his own life not long after leaving home at the young age of 25. I know he meant a lot to Shawna; of course, this was devastating.

Despite all that, Shawna has grown into a strong, beautiful woman, owns a business, and is a wonderful mother to four lovely children. She no longer has any contact with her mother or father. She sincerely apologized for everything I had endured.

Even though I never blamed her, and she was not the cause of my pain and suffering, hearing those words from her helped me release a tremendous amount of pent-up pain and the heavy burden I had carried for 25 years. It was as if I had been waiting all that time to hear them.

I didn't want her to feel guilty or live with an undeserved burden, and I reminded her that we were both just high school teenagers, and it was all in the past and a long time ago.

I want to honestly and sincerely apologize for this book's childish, immature insults and name-calling. I thought I could write about everything with my emotions under control, and I was hoping to be able to write like a gentleman.

Someone smarter than myself told me once, "If you handle every day and every situation like a gentleman, everyone else would have no choice but to treat you the same."

I guess I failed, and I am sorry.

Of course, I want to look perfect and irreproachable in front of the world and everybody, and I guess I could go back and airbrush my words and edit myself wonderfully, but the point of the book is to let people get to know the real me and judge me for the man I truly am.

Unfortunately, I am not perfect, and I am only human, made of flesh and bone, and sometimes my emotions are stronger than my will to be proper and correct. Well, that is my story, how I became the man I am today, and all the reasons my life is the way it is now.

If you are reading these words and are still rocking it out with me, you are fantastic, my friend. It means a lot to me, and I am grateful. I wish I had a more positive and educational reason for writing this book, something that could benefit all of humanity.

But as I mentioned at the beginning, I am just one out of billions of people on earth, each with a deeply personal story to pour out and share with the world to drink in. I hope you have enjoyed the taste of my life and its unique flavor. I hope the drink was not too bitter or too sweet.

Regardless of how my life tasted to you, we got through every drop together, and somehow, our new relationship is stronger, and we are all better for it, right? Who the fuck knows, I just don't know how to end a damn book?

THE END!!

T. LYTTON

DRINK IN ME

P.S. UPDATE:

The Final Fight Piece of Evidence

Not long after finishing this book, I found myself right back where I started —petitioning the court, again, to have my name removed from the sex offender registry.

This time, I did what the judge had suggested all those years ago. I hired a lawyer. I told myself that things were different now. A new sheriff was in office, time had passed, and after everything, surely there would be no issue this time. I should've known better. By law, I had to file my petition in Iredell County—the same place where this nightmare started.

And stupidly, I let myself hope that maybe, just maybe, enough time had passed for the corruption to have faded. But some stains never wash away. Years ago, when I first petitioned, the DA at the time didn't even object. She flat-out admitted that my case was complicated—that the law had been twisted and manipulated back in 1998. She could see the bullshit for what it was. And yet, despite her not fighting against me, the judge still denied my petition.

No explanation. No reasoning. Just denied. Fast forward to my second attempt.

This time, I walked into that courtroom with legal representation, believing that this would finally be it. But the DA across from me? Different person. Different agenda. And within minutes of that hearing starting, I knew—she had already made up her mind. She wasn't arguing facts.

She wasn't examining evidence. She was performing. Going through the motions of a decision that had already been made long before I even set foot in that room. And in that moment, it hit me. The system had never changed. It never intended to change.

I had already finished writing this book before I walked into that courtroom. I thought I had told the whole story. That I had laid it all out. But after sitting through that hearing, after watching history repeat itself in real time, I knew I had to include this final piece. Because words can be doubted. Stories can be questioned.

But this? This is the official record. This isn't my version of events. This is theirs. If you've read my story from start to finish, then this transcript will show you exactly what I have faced all these years. I'm not going to break it down for you.

I'm not going to explain it. Because I don't need to. The truth is in these pages. For those of you who have followed my story with an open mind—thank you. For those who questioned me, who thought maybe I had exaggerated, who weren't sure what to believe—I don't blame you. I understand.

That's why I'm letting this final part speak for itself. Read it. Judge it. Decide for yourself. Because at this point? I don't know what else to say.

NORTH CAROLINA GENERAL COURT OF JUSTICE

SUPERIOR COURT DIVISION

STATE OF NORTH CAROLINA		
		IREDELL COUNTY
v		98 CRS 022825
		98 CRS 022826
TIMOTHY LYTTON,		98 CRS 022827
Defendant		98 CRS 022828

TRANSCRIPT, Volume 1 of 1

(Pages 1-18)

Wednesday and Thursday, September 11-12, 2024

September 11, 2024, Criminal Session

HONORABLE JOSEPH N. CROSSWHITE, JUDGE PRESIDING

MOTION

APPEARANCES:

Regina Mahoney, Assistant District Attorney
203 Constitution Lane,
Statesville, NC 28677
Regina.m.mahoney@nccourts.org
       On behalf of the State

Jason Ralston, Esq.
335 N. Center St.
Statesville, NC 28677
jralston@rbbm.law.com
       On behalf of the Defendant

Rebecca Larsen, CVR
Official Court Reporter
PO Box 3044, Morganton, NC 28680
Rebecca.L.Larsen@nccourts.org

DRINK IN ME

1   I N D E X

2   Page

3   Motion by defense 3

4   State's objection 4

5   Defense's response 4

6   State's response 9

7   Defense's response 12

8   State's response 14

9   Court ruling 17

10

11

12

13

14

15

16

17

18

19

20

21

22

23

24

25

Rebecca Larsen, CVR
Official Court Reporter
rebecca.l.larsen@nccourts.org

```
 1                    P R O C E E D I N G S
 2                   (Began - 11:49 a.m.)
 3         (Defendant and all counsel were present.)
 4         MS. MAHONEY:  Your Honor, the next matter for the
 5   court is a write-on to this session.  The defendant's name
 6   is Timothy Lytton.  This is Mr. Ralston's petition for his
 7   client's removal from the sex offender registry.  The State
 8   is opposing that application.  I would ask to be heard when
 9   Mr. Ralston has completed his argument.
10         THE COURT:  Okay.  Thank you and --
11         MS. MAHONEY:  Would you like to see that court
12   file?
13         THE COURT:  I would.  And just a quick question for
14   you.
15         I know there's a couple of factors we have to
16   consider, most of them are just yes-or-no kind of things.  I
17   think there's one, factor number 6, that really is kind of a
18   discretionary thing.
19         Are you opposing it because he's not complied with
20   the other -- and I'll give you a chance to fully answer, but
21   I just want to know when I listen to Mr. Ralston.  Are you
22   -- are you opposing it because he's not complied with the --
23   the other requirements or because that you think he might be
24   still a potential threat or danger to the community?
25         MS. MAHONEY:  Your Honor, the State's opposing the
```

DRINK IN ME

1 petition on multiple grounds. The initial is one of

2 qualification. It's my position that one of the offenses

3 for which the defendant was convicted is a Tier III offense

4 for which removal early from the sex offender registry is

5 not available.

6 　　　　THE COURT: Okay.

7 　　　　MS. MAHONEY: So my objection is that he's not even

8 qualified to be filing the petition. And just -- Your

9 Honor, I'd just refer you to the prior judge's order from

10 December of 2020. That was the finding then, the first time

11 that Mr. Lytton had asked to be removed from the registry.

12 There's an order and finding that it was a Tier III offense

13 at that time.

14 　　　　I know that's a point of contention between

15 Mr. Ralston and myself and I -- I don't want to speak for

16 him.

17 　　　　THE COURT: Okay. Thank you.

18 　　　　MS. MAHONEY: But that's my position.

19 　　　　THE COURT: All right.

20 　　　　Mr. Ralston?

21 　　　　MR. RALSTON: Well, and -- and Judge, if the State

22 objects on several levels, maybe we should take the standing

23 issue first of whether he's even eligible, which I believe

24 comes down to the federal Wetterling Act portion of this

25 petition. And what I would say to that is the State is

1   going to allege, going to argue, that Mr. Lytton is what's

2   referred to as a "Tier III sex offender" pursuant to federal

3   statute, and I printed that out for Your Honor.

4   If I may approach?

5   THE COURT: Yes, sir.

6   MR. RALSTON: And I've got a copy. I don't know if

7   Ms. Mahoney has a copy, but if I may approach and I'll show

8   this to you.

9   THE COURT: Yes, sir, thanks.

10   (Unrelated court matter addressed.)

11   THE COURT: Yes, sir.

12   MR. RALSTON: And now in the -- in this portion of

13 the federal statutes where a sex offender is determined to

14 be -- be whether a Tier I sex offender, a Tier II sex

15 offender, or a Tier III sex offender, and it's listed here,

16 and the State is alleging, as you've heard and I think it's

17 the judge improperly found on the last -- on the last

18 petition that my client filed pro se -- found that he was a

19 Tier III sex offender.

20   Now, if you look at this statute, it -- when it

21 talks about a Tier III sex offender, it talks about a sex

22 offender that's punishable for imprisonment for more than

23 one year, comparable to more severe -- the following

24 offenses. And it lists some -- some federal statutes that

25 I've gone over with Ms. Mahoney and I don't think -- I do

DRINK IN ME

1   not think that she is -- objects or -- or feels that he

2   falls under those statutes, or if she does I'll come back

3   and argue those. But it really goes to B of that Tier III

4   sex offender that says the kidnapping -- or that the sex

5   offense involves a kidnapping of a minor.

6   Now, we filed this petition and I listed -- there

7   were four offenses that my client -- my client pled guilty

8   to back in 1999. Three were statutory rape, more than --

9   more than four, less than six, and second-degree kidnapping.

10   After speaking with Ms. Mahoney this morning, it's

11 come to my attention that he's not even required to register

12 for the rape offenses but just for the second-degree

13 kidnapping.

14   And the reason I would argue to Your Honor -- and I

15 would submit that this is not a Tier III sexual offense --

16 is because by statute and by definition -- and I have a copy

17 of the kidnapping statute. Unfortunately, I only printed

18 one.

19   If I may approach, Judge?

20   THE COURT: Yes, sir.

21   MR. RALSTON: To be an offense of second-degree

22 kidnapping what makes it a second-degree kidnapping is the

23 fact that the victim was returned to a safe space, that the

24 victim was not injured, and that the victim was not sexually

25 assaulted. So I would submit to Your Honor that his

1   conviction for second-degree kidnapping, although

2   registrable under the state statute, under the federal

3   tiering system it can't be a sexual offense that involves

4   kidnapping of a minor because the statute and what he pled

5   guilty to specifically says it did not involve sexual

6   assault.

7   THE COURT: Mm-hmm.

8   MR. RALSTON: So I do not think it fits as a Tier

9   III offense and therefore, we would submit to you that it is

10   a Tier I offense that would allow him to petition to be

11   removed early. But you simply can't have a sexual

12   offense -- you can't say that the second-degree kidnapping

13   is a sexual offense involving the kidnapping of a minor for

14   the tiering system in federal court when the state statute

15   for which he was convicted says there wasn't a sexual

16   assault.

17   THE COURT: Right. And let me ask you this, and

18   I'm -- because I did go back and I looked and I can see the

19   order from Judge Brooks back on December 8, 2020, and --

20   Mr. Ralston, I guess let me ask you this even just

21   preliminarily. We have a -- a finding and an order from

22   another Superior Court judge and I know one of the -- the

23   main rules that judges have to follow is we can't overrule

24   another judge. So does that kind of put me in the position

25   of doing that?

Rebecca Larsen, CVR
Official Court Reporter
rebecca.l.larsen@nccourts.org

1   MR. RALSTON: I don't believe so, Judge, because

2 the -- the removal -- the registration removal statute

3 allows for a new petition to be filed. I don't think the

4 Court is necessarily bound by a prior order.

5   THE COURT: Okay.

6   MR. RALSTON: I believe the, you know, being it's

7 not a res judicata issue because the statute specifically

8 allows a year later for a new petition to be filed and I

9 believe that you would take that as a de novo petition.

10   THE COURT: Right. Let me -- I'm gonna pull that

11 up in just a minute.

12   Ms. Mahoney, I -- give me one minute to pull this

13 up and I'm gonna give you a chance to be heard on this Tier

14 III --

15   MS. MAHONEY: Yes, sir.

16   THE COURT: -- but give me one minute if you don't

17 mind.

18   All right. Mr. Ralston, can you guys approach for

19 just a minute, please.

20   (Bench conference - 11:58 a.m.)

21   THE COURT: All right. We can go back on the

22 record. Just -- the Court, having showed this rule to the

23 attorneys in the article written by Michael Crowell as far

24 as one judge overruling another, that's gonna be something

25 I'm gonna want to spend a little bit more time with and see

T. LYTTON

1 if this follows the general rule or if it's one of the two

2 exceptions.

3   Mr. Ralston, I do think I understand your argument

4 as far as whether or not this is Tier III. I want to give

5 the State a chance to respond. I just want you both to

6 understand I'm gonna let you get your arguments on the

7 record, but I'm probably not gonna make a ruling now. I'm

8 probably gonna take it under advisement until I can --

9   MR. RALSTON: Absolutely.

10   THE COURT: -- spend a little bit more time with

11 it.

12   But Ms. Mahoney, as far as any argument on behalf

13 of the State as to whether or not this was a Tier III sex

14 offense.

15   MS. MAHONEY: Yes, Your Honor. The State's

16 position is that the second-degree kidnapping is a Tier III

17 offense. In the document that Mr. Ralston just handed up,

18 an excerpt from the federal statute under Tier III sex

19 offenders, subsection (b) it states "involve kidnapping of a

20 minor unless committed by a parent or guardian." That does

21 not -- in its plain meaning that does not require an

22 explicit statement that there's a sex offense.

23   I will note for the Court that the defendant was

24 indicted on three counts of statutory rape greater than four

25 years age difference, less than six, which is not

Rebecca Larsen, CVR
Official Court Reporter
rebecca.l.larsen@nccourts.org

DRINK IN ME

1 registrable, but he ended -- ultimately he pled to those

2 offenses and second-degree kidnapping, which is registrable.

3   I agree with Mr. Ralston in that the -- an analysis

4 of the elements of each crime is necessary in determining

5 whether it's a Tier I, Tier II, or Tier III. I will advise

6 the Court that the second-degree kidnapping statute in North

7 Carolina, 14-39, kidnapping, recites that if it's a

8 individual who's kidnapped, who's under the age of 16, the

9 State would have to state the purpose of the kidnapping, and

10 there are six subsections from which the State can choose.

11   We did not have the indictment or bill of

12 information from back in 1999 in the court file, so I cannot

13 state for the Court what was included within that

14 indictment, but I can tell the Court that the purpose is an

15 element and the only purpose here was sexual contact between

16 the two.

17   Your Honor, this was a 14-year-old victim at the

18 time and a 19-year-old defendant -- was he 18? Excuse me --

19 18 years old at the time. I can advise the Court that

20 although a 14-year-old cannot consent under law, they were

21 in a relationship.

22   So this is not a case where it's a forcible act or

23 where she was not released in a safe place on the kidnapping

24 charge after the encounter, so that's why it's

25 second-degree, because she was released. They were there

T. LYTTON

1   together for the sexual act. But the State would have had

2   to allege a purpose. The only purpose on the facts here

3   that exist was the sexual contact and encounter.

4   So it's my position that you don't need that; you

5   just need kidnapping of a minor per the federal statute, but

6   in the event that the Court believes that you need that as

7   an aspect of the crime, we have that here, too.

8   THE COURT: Okay.

9   MS. MAHONEY: So that's my argument why it should

10 be to Tier III. There was already a finding that it is a

11 Tier III, and under North Carolina law that's a

12 registration -- it's a 30-year registration. The only way

13 that can be reduced is if the defendant shows that he is in

14 compliance with the federal laws. Even though the federal

15 sentencing guidelines are different from the state's, it

16 still requires that he comply with the federal guidelines,

17 and the federal guidelines for a Tier III is a lifetime

18 registration.

19   So it's the State's position that the defendant

20 needs to stay registered for 30 years, exclusive of time in

21 custody, and then he can be removed from the registry but

22 not a day sooner.

23   THE COURT: Yes, ma'am. And -- so if I understand

24 you right, what you're saying is even if I take Mr.

25 Ralston's argument, he's still a Tier III. That's basically

1   what you're saying under the -- under your reading of the

2   statute, right?

3   MS. MAHONEY: It is, Your Honor, and that's in the

4   document that Mr. Ralston handed up to you.

5   THE COURT: Okay. Thank you.

6   MS. MAHONEY: It just says "involves kidnapping of

7   a minor."

8   THE COURT: Okay.

9   Mr. Ralston, we'll give you a chance to respond to

10 that.

11   MR. RALSTON: Yes, sir. And what I did hand you,

12 Judge, it starts off with terms and it talks about sex

13 offender, and it says, "the term 'sex offender' means an

14 individual who is convicted of a sex offense." So I don't

15 think, even under Tier III because it says, "involves

16 kidnapping of a minor child," there has to be someone

17 convicted of a sexual offense, that it -- that the

18 kidnapping -- it involved the kidnapping of a minor child.

19   When the Court looks at this, the Court can't

20 really take a factual analysis of what happened based on the

21 charges. It has to take an elemental one. It has to take

22 the elements of that crime and that's -- that's also in

23 the -- in the -- in the bench book as well, Judge.

24   But you have to look at the elements of the crime

25 and the elements of the kidnapping. The elements of the

T. LYTTON

1   thing that he is on the registration for, the second-degree
2   kidnapping, be it -- and I'm -- I'm not arguing that under
3   our state statute the second-degree kidnapping requires him
4   to register. What I'm saying is the elements of that
5   dictate that the victim was not sexually abused. So he
6   cannot be a sex offender and -- involving kidnapping of a
7   minor child when what's put him on the registry to begin
8   with says that didn't happen. You have to look at the
9   elements of it. We can't -- we can't go back and look
10 factually. And, of course, Ms. Mahoney and I, I think
11 talking to her earlier, we were both in law school when this
12 case was pled in, so neither one of us know what happened.
13 We don't have the indictment to see what was alleged and
14 there's several things that are alleged for kidnapping that
15 don't involve any -- any sexual act.
16   So we can't -- the Court can't infer that, it has
17 to look at the elements of the crime, and the elements says
18 it didn't happen.
19   THE COURT: Okay, so -- and -- and again, I mean,
20 looking at what you handed up, where it says "(b), involves
21 kidnapping of a minor," I mean, that's pretty simple. And I
22 understand what you're saying is that you got to look past
23 that, you got to look at the actual elements. Is there any
24 case law that you know of that says that or -- I mean,
25 because if -- I mean, if we just look at what's written here

DRINK IN ME

1   under (b), I mean, it seems pretty -- pretty

2   straightforward, but -- but your argument is you have to

3   look past that to the elements. And you may be right. I

4   just don't -- I don't know of that. I guess I'm asking if

5   you have any authority.

6   MR. RALSTON: I -- I don't, Judge. And really what

7   I'm saying is that it has to be a sexual offense. Under the

8   sex offender -- sex offender tiering, it has to be a sexual

9   offense and to be Tier III, that involves the kidnapping of

10   a minor child.

11   Well, the kidnapping that he was convicted of and

12   he pled to doesn't have a sexual -- as a matter of fact, it

13   says that the victim was not sexually abused, so he can't

14   be -- he can't be both under a second-degree kidnapping.

15   THE COURT: Okay.

16   MR. RALSTON: He can't be a sex offender that

17   involved a kidnapping when the second-degree kidnapping says

18   there was no sexual offense.

19   THE COURT: Okay. All right.

20   Ms. Mahoney, any final word on behalf of the State?

21   MS. MAHONEY: Yes, Your Honor, I just wanted to --

22   just wanted to -- just two quick points for the record. I

23   mean, if the child is a minor, it's sexual abuse. I mean,

24   you know, sexual contact with a minor cannot be consensual,

25   that's one point I want to make. The other is under the

T. LYTTON

1   state statutes, under the registration statutes, kidnapping
2   is classified differently from the other sexually violent
3   offenses, and I'm trying to find them now.
4   I know it's 14-208 -- I have it right here,
5   14-208.6 sub (1m) is offense against a minor. So one has
6   to -- one has to register in North Carolina if one commits
7   an offense against a minor and the statute is 14-29 [sic],
8   kidnapping and that's -- that's registrable. Separately are
9   listed all of the sexually violent offenses under sub (5).
10   So it's my position that a plain meaning reading of
11 this is that the two are separate classifications and the
12 kidnapping does not also require a sex offense component to
13 it. It's -- and I could -- I'm sure you have the -- the red
14 book up there, but in the definitions, they're -- they're
15 separate categories. I believe that was intentional because
16 the kidnapping of a minor alone would qualify.
17   THE COURT: Okay. Thank you.
18   Mr. Ralston, I'm gonna -- we're gonna -- I'm gonna
19 pause this because I have to go back and deal with those
20 other two people back in the office, but before I do I want
21 to give you a chance to get anything on the record. Again,
22 I'm not gonna get any kind of an order on the record now.
23 I'm gonna do it at some point.
24   MR. RALSTON: And I -- I understand, Judge, and I
25 guess just practically speaking, if that was the case, our

DRINK IN ME

1   statutes would specifically prohibit removal from the

2   registration for kidnapping, and I find it very difficult to

3   believe that you couldn't be removed from registration for

4   second-degree kidnapping but could for rape. It doesn't

5   make sense. They would specifically exclude it. It would

6   be -- even be on the AOC form if it did not involve

7   kidnapping and it's not because that's not a proper

8   interpretation.

9   THE COURT: Okay. All right. Well, why don't we

10   just -- let me put this matter -- let me just hold this open

11   for a while. Do you guys want to both be back in the

12   courtroom or do you just want an email with the ruling, or

13   how -- I mean, it will be within the next 24 hours.

14   MR. RALSTON: Email -- email's fine.

15   MS. MAHONEY: Your Honor, email's fine with us too.

16   THE COURT: Okay.

17   MS. MAHONEY: And then if it requires an additional

18   appearance, we'll coordinate.

19   THE COURT: Okay. All right, guys.

20   Well, thank y'all very much, and we'll be at ease

21   then until 2:00.

22   (Court recessed at 12:15 p.m. and reconvened

23   at 11:25 a.m. on Thursday, September 12,

24   2024.)

25   (Defendant and counsel were not present.)

Rebecca Larsen, CVR
Official Court Reporter
rebecca.l.larsen@nccourts.org

T. LYTTON

1   THE COURT: This is that hearing from yesterday.
2   I'm gonna -- we did the hearing. I said I wanted to review
3   the information, asked the parties if they wanted to be
4   here; it was Ms. Mahoney and Jason Ralston. They said they
5   did not, I could just notify them later, but I do want to
6   formerly get the order on the record.
7   This is in Timothy Daniel Lytton, 98 CRS 22825.
8   This was on for his motion to be released from the sex
9   offender registry. I have reviewed relevant case law, I
10 have reviewed Statute 14-39 concerning kidnapping, and I
11 have reviewed the rules for removal from the sex offender
12 registration. At this time, Court discretion will find that
13 this is a Tier III sex offense. The Court is taking the
14 plain meaning of the language; and since it is a Tier III
15 sex offense, the defendant's motion is denied.
16   So I'll call them both and I'll -- or I'll text
17 them both and I'll let them know.
18   Thank you very much.
19   (Proceedings concluded - 11:27 a.m.)
20
21
22
23
24
25

Rebecca Larsen, CVR
Official Court Reporter
rebecca.l.larsen@nccourts.org

DRINK IN ME

1   CERTIFICATION OF TRANSCRIPT

2

3   I certify that the foregoing transcript of

4   proceedings taken at the September 9, 2024, Session in

5   Iredell County Superior Court is a true and accurate

6   transcript of the proceedings as reported by me and

7   transcribed by me or under my supervision. I further

8   certify that I am not related to any party or attorney nor

9   do I have any interest in the outcome of this action.

10   This, the 27th day of January, 2025.

11

12

13

14   _Rebecca Larsen_

15   REBECCA LARSEN, CVR
     Official Court Reporter - Division V Rover
16   PO Box 3044
     Morganton, NC 28680
17   480-313-7447
     rebecca.l.larsen@nccourts.org

18

19

20

21

22

23

24

25

Rebecca Larsen, CVR
Official Court Reporter
rebecca.l.larsen@nccourts.org

Final Words:

I just have a few things to say before I close this out.

I have no idea how you feel about me, my story, or everything you've read. Hell, I'll probably never know what you think. But there are a few things I need to point out—just in case they got overlooked. The DA's own words left no room for doubt. Read the transcript, and one thing becomes clear— she backed herself into a corner. That day, she had two choices: she could have engaged with the legal argument and proven why I should stay on the registry, or she could have ignored the law, twisted facts, and blindly defended a broken system.

She chose the second option. By doing so, she left herself with only two possibilities: She knowingly upheld corruption, which makes her unfit for office. She was too incompetent to understand the legal argument, which also makes her unfit for office. There is no third option. Either she was a prosecutor who didn't understand the case, or she was one who didn't care. If she was competent, she would have addressed my lawyer's argument instead of dancing around it.

If she was ethical, she would have considered the facts instead of protecting an outdated ruling. Instead, she misstated my age, ignored the actual legal issue, and acted like the decision had already been made before we even stepped into that courtroom. A prosecutor should know the facts of the case they're arguing. If she didn't know the details, that means she was unprepared and incompetent.

If she did know and still twisted them, that means she deliberately misled the court. Either way, she had no business deciding people's futures.

The entire point of the hearing was to determine whether I should remain on the registry. The whole mess about me being classified as Tier III should have been an obvious mistake or a blatant abuse of power.

Yet, the DA argued as if it had some kind of merit, as if the decision had already been made before I even opened my mouth. She didn't argue like a lawyer fighting for justice. She argued like a bureaucrat enforcing a rule no one was allowed to question. And that raises the biggest question of all: Was she just blindly following orders, or was she protecting something bigger?

Because a fair, competent prosecutor would have said: Let's look at the facts. Let's see if justice is actually being served. She didn't. Instead, she argued with tunnel vision, defending a system that—even she had to know —was flawed. So by the end of that hearing, the DA had backed herself into a trap. If she knew the system was being misapplied but fought against me anyway, she was complicit in injustice.

If she didn't realize the law was being misapplied, she was unqualified for her job. Either way, she had no business holding that kind of power over someone's life. And that's the real tragedy of this entire situation—the justice system was never built to admit when it was wrong. I'll leave it to you, the reader. I don't need to tell you what to think. The transcript speaks for itself.

I won't call her corrupt. I won't call her incompetent. I don't have to. The facts are there, and any reasonable person can see what happened. The only real question is—how many other people have had their lives ruined by people like her? And how many more will?

If you've made it this far, then you've seen everything. You've read my story. You've walked through the years of struggle, injustice, and pain that shaped my life. And now, after reading the court transcript, you've seen the truth for yourself. I won't tell you how to feel about it. That's for you to decide.

But as for me? I'm still standing. There was a time when I thought justice was inevitable. That the truth would always rise to the surface. That good would always win in the end. But life has taught me otherwise.

Justice isn't guaranteed. Truth can be ignored. And sometimes, good people lose battles they never should've had to fight. But even knowing that, I refuse to let bitterness consume me. Yes, my life has been hard. Yes, I am tired.

Yes, I carry wounds that will never fully heal. But I am not broken. I won't give them that satisfaction. Because at the end of the day, I am more than what they tried to make me. I have seen the worst in people, but I have also seen kindness in places I never expected. I have been lied about, manipulated, and cast aside.

But I have also found strength I never knew I had. And that is what I choose to hold onto. I have to let go and move forward. I won't pretend forgiveness is easy. It's not. But I am choosing to let go of the hate. Not because they deserve it. But because I deserve peace.

I will not waste the rest of my life being angry at a system that refuses to change. I will not let resentment take up space in my heart when there is still so much more I want to do, so much more I want to be. I don't know what the future holds. But I know this: I will not let them define it.

And now, since they refuse to remove my name from the list this book will do it for for them. We all will do it for them. Because for every person that reads this and knows the truth the less power that list has and the more shame is placed on them and the courts.

And I will never stop fighting to be the man I was meant to be. This is not the end of my story. I don't know what's next, but I do know this much— I am still here. And I am still standing. To those who took the time to read this—thank you. Whether you believe me or not, whether you understand or not, whether you support me or not—I thank you for listening.

Because that's all I've ever wanted. To be heard. To be understood. To finally, after all these years, have my side of the story told. I can finally say it:

The truth really does set you free.

T. LYTTON

DRINK IN ME

---

www.ingramcontent.com/pod-product-compliance
Lightning Source LLC
Chambersburg PA
CBHW061012280326
41935CB00009B/936